Twayne's Filmmakers Series

Warren French
EDITOR

Lindsay Anderson

Lindsay Anderson

directing *The Singing Lesson* in Poland (1967)

Lindsay
Anderson

ALLISON GRAHAM

BOSTON

Twayne Publishers

1981

Lindsay Anderson

is first published in 1981 by Twayne Publishers,
A Division of G. K. Hall & Co.

Copyright © 1981 by G. K. Hall & Co.

Printed on permanent/durable acid-free paper and bound
in the United States of America

First Printing, November 1981

Library of Congress Cataloging in Publication Data

Graham, Allison.
Lindsay Anderson.

(Twayne's filmmakers series)
Outgrowth of the author's thesis (Ph. D—University of Florida)
Bibliography: pp. 159–62
Filmography: pp. 163–68
Includes index.
1. Anderson, Lindsay, 1923–
I. Title. II. Series.
PN1998.A3A584   791.43'0233'0924   81–4127
ISBN 0–8057–9283–X   AACR2

Contents

About the Author

Editor's Foreword

Preface

Acknowledgments

Chronology

1. New Identities, New Images   19

2. "Self-Delighting Liberty": The Documentaries   43

3. The Primal Politics of *This Sporting Life*   57

4. *The White Bus* and *The Singing Lesson:* Severed Roots and Tenuous Connections   83

5. *If . . . :* Exploding the "Protocol of Ancient Fatuity"   93

6. The Epic Structure of *O Lucky Man!:* New Identities, New Images   123

7. Afterword: British Possibilities, The Descending Spiral?   151

    Notes and References   153

    Selected Bibliography   159

    Filmography   163

    Index   169

About the Author

ALLISON GRAHAM was born in Florida, attended Florida State University, and received the Ph.D. in English and Film Studies from the University of Florida (where her dissertation was on the major films of Lindsay Anderson). She is a member of the faculty of the Department of Theatre and Communication Arts at Memphis State University.

Editor's Foreword

ALLISON GRAHAM calls *If . . .* , I believe justifiably, "one of England's most original contributions to world cinema." At the same time, she refutes the criticism that has confused this unique film with the now rather dated American films of the late 1960s and early 1970s about rebellious youth, like *The Strawberry Statement* and *Medium Cool*. Anderson was not taking advantage of a trend of the times, as even Michelangelo Antonioni was in *Zabriskie Point,* to score at the box office. (As a matter of fact, few of the "youth revolt" films from the years of unrest on college campuses between 1968 and 1970 made large profits.) *If . . .* is entirely consistent in style and theme with the very few other feature films that Lindsay Anderson has directed, the keystone of his unremitting attack on middle-class respectability, especially as embodied in the English Establishment.

Though now nearing sixty, Anderson has made fewer feature films than almost any other major auteur except Jean Vigo, whose surrealistic *Zéro de Conduite* is also frequently used comparatively to oversimplify Anderson's far more complex and apocalyptic *If . . .* In part, as Allison Graham explains, Anderson's limited output can be attributed to the lamentable decline in British film production during the 1970s. The nation that in the 1930s established itself internationally as one of the most important sources of film art with the early (and still best) Hitchcock thrillers and Alexander Korda's productions like *The Private Life of Henry VIII* and *Rembrandt,* reached even greater heights after World War II with an unparalleled run of masterful comedies. For just a little more than a decade from 1949 to 1960, British films—many produced and directed by the Boulting Brothers, many starring Alec Guinness or Ian Carmichael— set a standard that has not been matched anywhere else and probably never will be—with delights like *Passport to Pimlico* (1949), *Kind Hearts and Coronets* and *The Happiest Days of Our Life* (both 1950),

Genevieve (1954), *Private's Progress* (1956), *Lucky Jim* and *The Horse's Mouth* (both 1958), and *I'm All Right, Jack* (1960). The Vikings who invade the television station at the bitter end of this last prophetic film mentioned seem indeed to have taken over, for British films have lost the impish innocence that perhaps only the 1950s could have fostered, while a declining world market has cut British production to a minimum.

In some ways, however, this reversal of national fortunes has not been entirely hurtful to Lindsay Anderson. He has actually worked much more as a director in the theater than for the cinema; and he has produced commercials for television, like many other distinguished British artists. His ventures in these more transient media have been much more diverse than his films, and this display of the variety of his talents especially focuses attention upon the single-mindedness of his cinematic fictions—the short *The White Bus* and the three features, *This Sporting Life*, *If . . .* , and *O Lucky Man!* Had he been obliged to turn out one film after another, he could scarcely have dealt with such intensity with the convulsions of a decadent society that refuses to die, so that the British spiril might enjoy a jubilant aesthetic reincarnation of the kind fantasied at the end of *O Lucky Man!* (Even in their salad days, the geniuses of British comedy were responsible for not only triumphs like *The Titfield Thunderbolt* and *The Lady-Killers*, but also for the "Carry On" series and *An Alligator Named Daisy*.)

Anderson is thus one of those few lucky men who has had the opportunity to concentrate on doing singularly well what he can do singularly well. If the scope of his cinema has been limited to an in-depth exploration of twentieth-century depersonalization and de-humanization, these few films display an unvarying power that makes each of his works truly his best. As Allison Graham points out, despite his discontent with crumbling institutions, Anderson has never had a political ax to grind; he has never limited his work by affiliating with narrow causes, but has persisted in calling for a celebration of the spontaneous creativity of the human race.

Since I first sat entranced though *If . . .* , I have never doubted Anderson's place in a series of this kind dedicated to those who have transformed commercial cinema into a powerful art form. Nothing remains so clearly in my mind as a visual symbol of Thoreau's concept of the incapacitating hold of the past on the present as that scene before the final apocalypse in *If . . .* when the school's dusty attic is emptied of its moldering treasures.

Allison Graham has, in this book, caught exactly the spirit in which Anderson made his films and has illuminated it for those who should also share it (our students should be assured regular access to these works). Her effort has been aided by the director himself, who has shared his thoughts and even memorable stills from his private collection with her for use in this book. With his cooperation we have thus been able to produce here the kind of book that we wish about the kind of artist we especially wish to celebrate.

W. F.

Preface

ALTHOUGH MY ORIGINAL intention was to write a fairly straightforward formalistic analysis of Lindsay Anderson's films, I found that as the project grew from dissertation to book form it seemed to acquire some fascinating cultural implications. Like all good films, of course, Anderson's do not require social or cultural interpretation to be intelligible, but even a minimal understanding of certain aspects of British culture—imperialism, social classes, regional differences and rivalries (especially those between "the English" and the "the British," which Anderson always mentions), and the obsession with royalty and history—can expand our appreciation significantly. Anderson's own passion for understanding his countrymen is a fact which simply cannot be overlooked, and whatever cultural biases appear in this study, it should be remembered that they stem primarily from the director's well-publicized pronouncements over the past three decades.

Since I do not claim to be an expert on British popular culture, my emphasis is always on the films themselves as visual experiences; most "extra-film" references are made to enhance the immediate appreciation of the works. Elizabeth Sussex's *Lindsay Anderson* (1969) deals extensively with Anderson's early career and writings, and several books (notably, Lovell and Hillier's *Documentary Explorations* and Alexander Walker's *Hollywood UK*) competently examine Anderson's role in Free Cinema, so that I have not felt compelled to reexplore these aspects of his life in great detail. Instead, I have focused on the process of Anderson's career, and have organized the book chronologically, movie by movie, to reflect his progressive involvement in artistic responses to social and political issues and increasing concern with the difficulty of creating "new identities" and "new images" in a class-bound society.

Chapter 1 discusses Anderson's place in the postwar English film tradition, reviews his political and aesthetic ideas from 1948 to 1980, and analyzes the consistent attitudes and themes in his films. Chapter 2 focuses on his documentary work from the late 1940s to 1957 and offers several reasons for the inevitability of his move to fiction filmmaking in 1963. The last chapters examine Anderson's most prolific period, the decade between 1963 and 1973, with the emphasis on his growing discontent with old forms of narration and tired approaches to such problems as class struggle, alienation, intellectualism, and rebellion. While Anderson's feature work began in the bleakest fictional milieu (the grimy rowhouses of *This Sporting Life*), it ended in the most glittering (the cast dance of *O Lucky Man!*), and the story of this evolution is as intimately connected to the social upheavals of that decade as it is to Anderson's maturation as a film artist. Thus chapter 3 looks at the "Angry" period of British filmmaking and finds *This Sporting Life* to be significantly different from other "kitchen sink" films of the time—an initial exploration of social, psychological, and (most interestingly) artistic constriction rather than a one-shot appeal to contemporary taste. Chapter 4 analyzes Anderson's two short films of the mid-1960s, *The White Bus* and *The Singing Lesson*, from this same perspective, while chapter 5 explores the making of *If . . .* , the interpretive problems it raised for critics at the time of its release, and its relationship to the rest of Anderson's work. Although most critics believe *If . . .* is Anderson's most interesting (and most "revolutionary") film, I find *O Lucky Man!* more complex, more deeply concerned with the basic issues of art in general—and film art in particular. As chapter 6 makes clear, Anderson's last major feature film (excluding *In Celebration*, which was the 1975 film version of David Storey's play) is truly the culmination of a career-long fascination with social, psychological, and artistic *change*. The final chapter offers some thoughts on Anderson's future work and the current state of British film.

To have grown up in an era saturated with British popular culture has made the demise of its once exuberant film tradition seem particularly sad, and I can only hope that a film like *Quadrophenia* is heralding some kind of rebirth of national spirit. The uniqueness of an artist like Anderson, however, has been his astounding ability to work *in spite of* economic realities and cultural prejudices, and to create some of the best films in the world.

Memphis, Tennessee

Acknowledgments

I WISH to thank a number of people who made completion of this book possible: Steve Snyder, for his encouragement and assistance; Warren French, for his consistently helpful and intelligent suggestions; Gary Sweet, for delivering *The White Bus* from North American oblivion and generously sharing his information; John Tilley and Susan Fisher of United Artists, for managing to arrange a screening of *The White Bus* in the midst of the New York Transit Strike; the Museum of Modern Art, for their efficiency and courtesy in arranging a screening of *Thursday's Children*; and Jill Hague and Stephen Phillips, for their help in getting around London. The research would never have been completed, though, without the incredible generosity of Lindsay Anderson himself, who not only arranged screenings in London of films I had been trying to locate for years, but spared a good deal of time to talk and correspond with me. I would especially like to thank him for allowing me to use stills from his personal collection. Such graciousness is rare indeed. Lyrics to Alan Price's songs "O Lucky Man!" and "Poor People" copyright © 1973 Keith Prowse Music Publishing Company Limited/Jarrow Music Limited. All Rights Reserved. Used by Permission of Warner Bros. Music.

Chronology

1923   Lindsay Anderson born in Bangalore, South India, 17 April.

1941   One year at Oxford while doing preofficer training.

1943–   Serves in Army (60th King's Royal Rifle Groups and Intelli-
1946   gence Corps).

1947   Begins to edit *Sequence*.

1948   Makes first film, an industrial documentary for Richard Sut-
       cliffe Ltd. entitled *Meet the Pioneers*, and graduates from
       Oxford (MA degree).

1949   Makes second industrial documentary, *Idlers That Work*, for
       Sutcliffe.

1952   Publishes *Making a Film: The Story of "Secret People,"* acts in
       James Broughton's *The Pleasure Garden*, makes *Three In-
       stallations* (for Sutcliffe) and *Wakefield Express*, and edits the
       last issue of *Sequence*.

1953   Directs *Thursday's Children* and *O Dreamland*.

1954   Makes *Trunk Conveyor*, his fourth and last industrial film for
       Sutcliffe.

1955   *Thursday's Children* wins Academy Award for Best Short
       Subject. Organizes season of John Ford films at the National
       Film Theatre, begins directing episodes for the television
       series *Robin Hood*, and makes a number of government-
       sponsored short films: *Green and Pleasant Land, Henry, The
       Children Upstairs, A Hundred Thousand Children, £20 a
       Ton, Energy First*, and *Foot and Mouth*.

1956   Organizes first Free Cinema Program at the National Film
       Theatre and supervises the editing of Lorenza Mazzetti's
       Together.

1957   Makes *Every Day Except Christmas* and directs first play at
       the Royal Court Theatre, *The Waiting of Lester Abbs. Every*

Day Except Christmas wins Grand Prix at the Venice Film Festival.

1958   Helps direct *March to Aldermaston* and becomes the film's major editor.

1959– Artistic director of the Royal Court Theatre.
1960

1959– Directs a number of plays in London: *The Long and the Short*
1961   and *the Tall, Billy Liar, Sergeant Musgrave's Dance, Progress to the Park, The Lily White Boys, Trials by Logue*, and *The Fire Raisers*.

1963   Makes *This Sporting Life*, and the film is the official British entry at the Cannes Film Festival. Directs Richard Harris on the stage in *The Diary of a Madman*.

1964   Directs *Andorra* and *Julius Caesar* for the London stage.

1966   Makes *The White Bus* and directs two plays, *The Cherry Orchard* in England and *Inadmissible Evidence* at the Contemporary Theatre, Warsaw.

1967   Makes *The Singing Lesson (Raz Dwa Trzy)* in Poland.

1968   Directs *If . . .* ; the film wins the Golden Palm at Cannes.

1969   Directs David Storey's plays *In Celebration* and *The Contractor* in London. *T.V. Mail* names him Director of the Year.

1969– Member of the Board of Governors of the British Film Insti-
1970   tute. In 1970 he and Karel Reisz resign in protest of certain BFI practices.

1970   *International Film Guide*'s Director of the Year. Directs Storey's play *Home* in New York.

1971   Directs televised production of *Home* for WNET, New York. Directs Storey's *The Changing Room*.

1973   Makes *O Lucky Man!*; the film is the official British entry at Cannes. Directs Storey's play *The Farm*.

1974   Directs Storey's *Life Class*.

1975   Directs *In Celebration* for the American Film Theater; and the plays *What the Butler Saw, The Sea Gull*, and *The Bed Before Yesterday* in London.

1977   The National Film Theatre features an Anderson exhibit entitled "The Thirty Years' War." Directs the play *The Kingfisher*.

1978   Directs video production of Alan Bennett's *The Old Crowd* for London Weekend Television.

1980   Directs Storey's play *Early Days* in London.

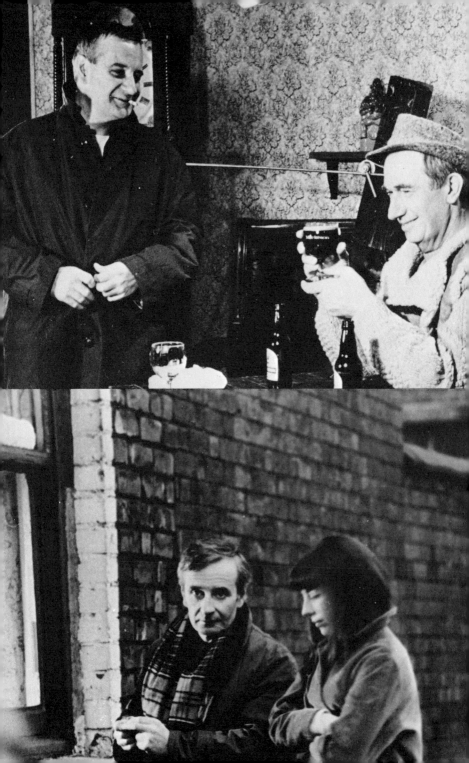

1

New Identities, New Images

"WE ARE STILL between Arnold's two worlds," Lindsay Anderson wrote in 1957, "one dead and the other powerless to be born." There is no question where the Old World lay: in that flickering image of "a country without problems in which no essential changes have occurred for the last fifty years, and which still remains the centre of an Empire on which the sun will never have the bad manners to set." But if his conviction seemed to be bitter rhetoric for an era steeped in the thick brew of liberal passion, he found justification in the movies: "In 1945, it is often said, we had our revolution. It is true we had something; though for a revolution it was a little incomplete. According to the British cinema, however, nothing happened at all. . . . What we need to consider is the image of ourselves that our cinema is bent on creating, and whether we, as a nation, should continue to accept that image."[1]

The creation of a new film tradition should have generated the imaginative power to propel England toward that luminous hinterland of new identities and images. The industry flirted with the prospect for several years, tentatively pulled up anchor, tacked and drifted a bit, but finally creaked back to shore. The moorings of tradition had only been frayed, not cut, and perhaps from the snug harbor of tired visions and genteel poverty the sun still seemed to set within the Empire. But not to Anderson, and it is a fair assessment of his renegade vision to say that it charted a course far into the imaginative topography that lay beyond the perimeters of New Wave sensibility.

To extend the nautical metaphor would only further accentuate the rather astounding fusion of England's geography and cultural spirit: the thing and its expression are very nearly one. Islanded by nature and obsessed with the past, the nation has often given the impression of resisting that manic acceleration of experience of the mid-

Anderson at work: (top) directing Bernard Mills in a commercial for Mackeson's Stout; (bottom) directing Patricia Healey in The White Bus *(1966)*

twentieth century. The lurid panorama of revolutions, assassinations, and other political pyrotechnics has for the most part remained "out there"—across the Channel, beyond the Atlantic, more a mural to contemplate than an invitation to participate. If in the 1950s Anderson was urging the English to "evolve new social relationships within the nation, and a new relationship altogether with the world outside," [2] he had, by the end of the 1970s, pretty much accepted the fact that this evolution would not occur: "The English—even more than the British generally—have strait-jacketed themselves with a class system that has made it impossible for them to develop a new national psychology to replace the psychology of Empire which inspired them for at least a hundred years." [3]

Anderson was not the only filmmaker who realized that breaking the seal of cultural hermeticism would involve dealing with one overriding reality: namely, that "everything in Britain has to be seen, at least partly, in 'Class' terms." But the attempts of the Free Cinema directors in the late 1950s and early 1960s to make "classless" films (or at least films which consciously debunked the class structure) resulted in works which now seem haunting reminders of what *might* have been: a film tradition which could capitalize on its unique position as neither American nor continental, neither "respectably bourgeois" nor "vulgarly 'popular' " [4] as their forebears had been (according to Anderson), but youthfully irreverent and imaginative, and for the most part willing to tackle adult subjects with true flair. For all their energy, though, these films represented only minor revolutions in the British film sensibility. The descendants and mutations of John Osborne's Jimmy Porter were never able to effect any real change, being elevated into the Sunday supplement pantheon of New Wave antiheroes all too easily. "The upper class in Britain is always so clever," Anderson noted in 1966. "It possesses a unique talent for assimilating disturbing elements." And maybe this is because some of these fashionable films of the 1960s were only "bourgeois assessments of the bourgeois situation. . . . They never go to causes, or imply the necessity of a real disruption, a real destruction of the society which has produced them." [5]

Anderson's fondness for such rhetoric has helped to foster an image of him as a politically radical director, but although he has always been highly attuned to political realities—or "causes"—he also has never relinquished his belief in *artistic* solutions. When he claims that "essentially, the failure of British Cinema is the failure of national self-belief," [6] he is really talking about the need to free oneself from political and cultural limitations. "Self-belief" is, if anything, a nonpolitical stance, a declaration of freedom from imposed points of view: it is at the heart of all of his characters' problems, and even England itself becomes a metaphor for *inherited* beliefs. To escape the weight of the past, to liberate oneself from social definition, to realize that one does not just peer out (or down) at others but is *peered at* in return, is to create a "new identity" and certainly a "new image." Even the concept of "self" changes when this happens (as it does over the course of Anderson's films); his treatment of character, in fact, seems to grow away from an interest in psychological complexity toward a Zen-like concern with *loss* of psychological depth and definition (witness the progression from Frank Machin of *This Sporting Life* to Michael Travis at the end of *O Lucky Man!*). Openness to the world is the key, it seems, and it is easy to share Anderson's exasperation with so many of the cheeky, seemingly irreverent "Angry" heroes of the 1960s, for their energies were for the most part squandered in obsessions with the social system (through madness, like Morgan in *Morgan: A Suitable Case for Treatment*, or resentment, like Arthur Seaton in *Saturday Night and Sunday Morning*).

An amazing fact about this period of filmmaking in England is that of the major directors involved, only Anderson has, in his words, "persisted in the faith," not turning to "conformist money-making or to emigration." [7] His relatively small output of films is a testament to this, for he has "only ever been able to function well in conditions of freedom" [8] (and artistic freedom, one must remember, does not mean simply the niceties of democracy to Anderson—it means being "a monster" whose duty it is "to bite the hand that feeds him" and "aim beyond the limits of tolerance").[9] Because of this, there is in his films a consistently imaginative process of experiment and discovery, a process all the more remarkable in light of the "extremely up-hill labour" [10] involved.

The Roots of Exploration

In the summer of 1977 Anderson was asked to organize a self-portrait at London's National Film Theatre. He originally called the exhibit "Thirty Years of Work," but later changed it to "The Thirty Years' War." Anyone familiar with his work or public personality would find this emendation absolutely appropriate, especially since the director himself was behind it. For Anderson, his work *has been* his war, his career a "fighting commitment," so much so that his reputation seems rooted in strange comminglings of military and pedagogical metaphors: he has been called a "good guerrilla" who could "travel light, go hungry, live frugally, and above all shed blood with no regret if it served the cause"; a testy "schoolmaster";[11] and even (by John Grierson) one of those "intellectual Teddy Boys" [12] of the fifties.

Ironically, Anderson grew up in an atmosphere most congenial to the entrenched conventions of the military and upper-middle-class education. He was born in an outpost of the Empire—Bangalore, India—in 1923, where his father was stationed with the Royal Engineers. He was educated in public schools in the south of England (one, Cheltenham College, became the setting for *If . . .*) and studied classics at Oxford in 1941 while enrolled in preofficer training. He served in the 60th Rifles and the Intelligence Corps from 1943 to 1946, then returned to Oxford to major in English and graduate with an M.A. in 1948.

When Anderson began to write criticism for *Sequence* (formerly the magazine of the Oxford University Film Society) in 1947, he—by sheer "luck" he often says—got the chance to make industrial documentaries for a Yorkshire factory manager. Although he had been a great fan of movies in college, had been a member of the Oxford University Film Society, and had acted in several university drama productions, he knew almost nothing about filmmaking. Nevertheless, when the wife of Desmond Sutcliffe (manager of Richard Sutcliffe, Ltd., a conveyor belt factory) asked him to make a documentary about the factory, he accepted, and ended up making four films for the firm, all in the North, and another on their recommendation for the centennial of a Yorkshire newspaper (*Wakefield Express*). He learned to make films by making films: even the subject of these documentaries is work itself—how things are made, how processes are set in motion. That he was writing a good deal of film criticism at this time—constantly doing and thinking—shows just how far he carried his own film education. By the time he finished this "apprenticeship" period around 1954, he began to find (and get funding for) his own projects. His criticism from this period (for *Sequence* and *Sight and Sound*) is still his most cogent: now that he was making films, his impatience with the mediocrity and prescriptive narrative style of most British films of the time was even more keen. His was the voice heard most often—and most clearly—in the pre–Free Cinema rumblings.

Anderson's critical belligerence has received a great deal of attention over the years, but a certain romanticism about either his temperament or the ethos of the "Angry decade" has often shrouded the exact nature of the war itself. To some, it has been a nonconformist's crusade against the commercial system; to others, it has been more of a social war, with Anderson cast as the standard bearer of kitchen sinks, realism, liberalism, and many other isms associated with postwar England. Surely it has been all of these at one time or another. Before he ever made a feature film, he was a leader of Free Cinema in the fifties (he coined the phrase, wrote most of the propaganda, directed the greatest percentage of documentaries in the programs), a major contributor to film journals, an actor, a television director, and an established theater director. For a man so many people view as the most influential filmmaker in postwar England, he has lived through a fair share of social and cultural battles, and they are important here insofar as they have impinged on or shaped artistic freedom or created specific problems which have warranted imaginative response. But the real "war" has been played out on a more personal level, and has centered on his struggles with the medium itself, those constant strivings to, as Anderson says, "try and find the single image that implies everything, instead of trying to make the film that contains everything specifically."[13]

Getting back to those quasi-military descriptions of Anderson, we might agree that the consistent recurrence of such terminology over a period of three decades could reveal a surprisingly legitimate response to his films. "It is only the bourgeois audience," he says, "or the bourgeois critics who imagine that thought is the enemy of feeling. As a Scot, I am much more familiar with the idea of passionate thought."[14] To unify, or harmonize, thought and feeling, instead of capitulating to a relatively easy sentimentality or intellectualism, has always been a goal of his works and has always galvanized his role in "The Thirty Years' War," as well it might. For this search for integration and unity is anything but compatible with a culture whose two main obsessions are its social classes and glorious past.

Given Anderson's antipathy to such interests, and his acute awareness of the virtual impossibility of both persisting in his "faith" and getting the funding to make personal films in such an environment, one might wonder why he never emigrated. Gavin Lambert, who with Anderson founded *Sequence* in 1947, claims that "Lindsay has always been much more 'British' than I. He is impatient and sometimes furious, but remains deeply attached. He will always live there, I guess, because like [John] Ford he loves the idea of solid, far-reaching roots. . . . Lindsay will never desert his own past."[15]

To claim that someone who has spent decades raging against

"good-old-English Philistinism" [16] and middle-class complacence, and who has said he would have to be a "maniac" [17] to find the world a satisfactory place, is "deeply attached" seems, to put it mildly, contradictory. But there is really no contradiction. Anderson has always used Forster's words—"only connect"—to convey what he thinks movies do best: make connections. A simple enough thing to say, but what is really meant by "making connections"? To begin with, the attitudes he has baffled for so long—philistinism, bourgeois values, "tepid humanism," [18] fashionable liberalism—are obvious examples of false connections, attachments to ideas which have nothing to do with reality (especially the reality of a nation like England which has undergone such radical changes in status and economy), and there is nothing contradictory in his reviling attitudes which only degrade the country's positive qualities. The connections he values are those he has found in Ford's movies and which he himself sought out in his early documentaries: affection and community expressed *concretely*, without reference to class, family background, or biographical information of any sort—immediate, spontaneous contact:

[Ford's] vision is rounded by its emphasis on the relations of men with one another and with the world in which they find themselves; on life lived in community; on all the hazards and rewards of physical existence. The scenes of action in these films thus become something more than mere occasions for excitement; they reflect a philosophy that finds virtue in activity, seeing struggle as a necessary element in life. [19]

But how is Lambert's claim that Anderson cherishes "solid, far-reaching roots" manifested in his films? To be sure, no main character even possesses a visible family, much less any kind of "meaningful" connection with his environment. Frank Machin, in *This Sporting Life* (1963), tries desperately to make spiritual connections and fails; Mick Travis is socially connected to his environment in *If . . .* (1968), but hardly in a fruitful way—he, in fact, severs that connection at film's end by shooting down the officials and patrons of his school. In Anderson's two short films of the sixties, the same kinds of estrangement can be found: the girl in *The White Bus* (1966) returns to her northern hometown to find nothing but a pervasive detachment and loneliness, and while the music students in *The Singing Lesson* (1967) have a family of sorts in their classroom, they are dissociated in every way from the people outside the school. Michael Travis, in *O Lucky Man!* (1973), is, of course, the most

Detachment and Loneliness: Patricia Healey in The White Bus *(top); (bottom) family breakdown in* In Celebration *(Alan Bates at left, Constance Chapman, James Bolam).*

bizarrely detached from his world: every connection he thinks he makes is illusory. Only when he begins to connect with people on an imaginative level does he feel any sense of community; even the intense communal spirit of Anderson's documentaries is reborn here at the end of the film, in the exuberant cast dance.

Anderson's 1975 film version of David Storey's *In Celebration* for the American Film Theater is his only film which deals explicitly with the breakdown of family relationships. But even here (as in the film and novel versions of Storey's *This Sporting Life*) *familial* estrangement mirrors *social* estrangement. The family reunion, ostensibly a celebration of the parents' fortieth wedding anniversary, is an obvious sham, for there is little reason to celebrate a way of life which has lost all emotional and social validity. Although the three sons make radically different attempts to free themselves from their class-conscious, inhibition-ridden childhoods, the psychological divisions created by industrialism defeat them. They simply cannot integrate their awareness of a relatively unrestricted world with their knowledge of their father's hopelessly constricted one. The pull of the past is too strong, the guilt too great; they find themselves in limbo, unable to adjust to the new world, incapable of accepting the old one. The end of the play suggests that if such divisiveness cannot be resolved, one can at least give up an obsession with it and simply accept people as individuals, regardless of their entrapment within social and emotional limitations.

This process of acceptance which extends over six films is one of the most complex in Anderson's work, for it grows out of a rich mixture of social and philosophical issues and can be approached in a variety of ways. Certainly, his characters are all, in some ways, "victims of society," or more precisely, embodiments of that "failure of national self-belief," whose stories do nothing to bolster that hierarchy Anderson once described as "the self-idealized *elite* of class and wealth, the docile middle-classes, and the industrious devoted army of workers."[20] Whatever the class, his characters usually find no fulfillment or mobility within their social environments: Machin, the miner-turned-footballer, lives in as warped and inbred a world as the upper-middle-class Mick Travis. That none of these characters even so much as mentions his family implies *by omission* as much dissociation as hours of Pinteresque family squabbles. What far-reaching roots can there be for these people, who begin every film dispossessed of their families and any kind of regional or communal spirit?

While it may, again, seem odd that someone as emotionally tied to his country as Anderson would make movies about the *absence* of kinship, if most of the social arrangements one sees are antiquated or obsolete (if not downright corrupt), then the death of the family becomes not only the most appropriate metaphor for the situation, but a way of "wiping the slate clean" and starting anew. This is at the heart of his characters' problems: they are all thrust out on the screen with nothing but their own physical and imaginative resources; in a sense, they are pure, uninhibited images, each, as Maurice Merleau-Ponty would say, a consciousness "thrown into the world, subject to the gaze of others and learning from them what it is."[21] Yet so often they reject this liberation, either from fear (like Machin) or from lack of imagination (like Travis in *O Lucky Man!*), and try to burrow into any situation which holds out the illusion of security. (Mick Travis, in *If . . .* , is an obvious example of someone who overthrows such security, but ends up having nothing else to embrace, except pseudo-revolutionary rhetoric.)

The Stirrings of Discontent: Free Cinema and Early Criticism

Anderson's reputation as a political, or leftist, director seems to be based on his outspoken criticism from the fifties ("A hangover," he says, "from the early days of making documentary films and propaganda for Free Cinema").[22] In contrast to some of the major film movements—the French New Wave or Italian Neorealism, for example—Free Cinema was not particularly successful or influential ("a dwarf movement," [23] one author has called it), or even revolutionary (Karel Reisz claims it was a reaction, not a revolution). But in terms of British postwar culture it had a significant role in the apprenticeship of directors like Anderson, Reisz, and Tony Richardson, and was one of the few signs that Britain was tuned in to the European renaissance of the fifties (foreign directors like Polanski, Truffaut, Chabrol, Goretta, and Tanner had some of their films shown at the Free Cinema programs and Goretta claimed in 1977 that the Swiss film tradition would not have been possible without the help of Free Cinema). Anderson himself thought up the name "Free Cinema" for its publicity value, so that "the journalists would have an *idea* to write about and not just a cinema programme. Without that declamatory title, I honestly believe the Press would have paid us no attention at all . . . it was a successful piece of cultural packaging."[24] (He had actually thought up the title years before when he rewrote the last paragraph of an article submitted to *Sequence* by Alan Cooke.)

The films shown in the programs at the National Film Theatre from 1956 to 1959 had not been made specifically for Free Cinema. As Anderson says, " 'Free Cinema' was nothing more than a label of convenience. . . . It was never planned as anything other than a way of showing our work. It was pragmatic and opportunistic."[25] *O Dreamland* (1953) was in the first program in 1956; it had been made independently by Anderson for less than one hundred pounds. *Wakefield Express* (1952) and *Every Day Except Christmas* (1957) were shown in 1957.

Much has been written about Free Cinema and its attempts to inject into British cinema some sense of national realities, and these missions are usually seen as part of the great ascension of the working class. But Gavin Lambert had it right when he reviewed the first program for *Sight and Sound*: "Isolation of the individual, isolation of the crowd, isolation of escape—this is what one senses behind the Free Cinema programme."[26] Taken as a group, these films (which include Anderson's documentaries, Richardson's and Reisz's *Momma Don't Allow*, Reisz's *We Are the Lambeth Boys*, and Lorenza Mazzetti's *Together*) form a barely cohesive social image; it is, in fact, an image splintered into myriad fragments, connected only by the tenacious spirit of the filmmakers. These connections are only found, though, *within* the isolated groups, not *among* them, and here again is a reminder of the depth of social division in England, a clear indication that *intra*relatedness would have to suffice for the moment, *inter*relatedness being a rather impossible ideal. (And there are those who feel that these divisions were so much a part of the directors' Oxbridge psyches that they, unlike many Italian Neorealists, could never be true explorers of the subproletariat.) Yet any integrative process, like the one Anderson began in these films, must begin with inner harmony before it can extend to embrace the rest of society, and in this respect the Free Cinema films are significantly linked to the rest of Anderson's work (especially *This Sporting Life*, which for all its social bleakness is primarily about one man's failure to become spiritually self-sufficient).

Free Cinema was not political in any specific sense. As Anderson says, "Implicit in the critical or radical social attitudes of those films was a belief in the possibility of reform, there was a belief in the necessity of change, in the possibility of change—in a word, an idealism."[27] To understand the significance of Free Cinema one should see it not only as a well-orchestrated publicity maneuver for the Young Turks of British cinema but as part of the general climate of change which characterized that period of British culture.

The resurgence of drama and film which began in 1956 with Richardson's production of *Look Back in Anger*, Free Cinema, and the visit of Brecht's Berliner Ensemble was probably inevitable, according to Anderson: "The time was historically ripe for a breakthrough of both creative and social activity in the flabby, exhausted atmosphere of postwar Britain."[28] Yet the "angry movement" was in some ways another journalistic exaggeration of "a period of what we might call radical breakthrough of which Free Cinema was a part" (the adjective "angry" having been used to label nearly any artist with vaguely anti-status quo leanings).

Anderson feels that Free Cinema introduced "certain imaginative principles" into British cinema, the "breaking down of bourgeois restrictions of theme and style"[29] being by far the most important. And here, too, Free Cinema was in harmony with the strides being taken in the theater. To read the Free Cinema program notes (written by Anderson) is really to read an encapsulated history of the artistic temperament of the fifties. Given Anderson's connections with nearly every aspect of the British cultural establishment (and antiestablishment), there should be no surprise at this. What is surprising, though, is the extent to which one man shaped this ethos, for these proclamations are the culmination of every principle Anderson had been fighting for since he began his career in 1947. "No film can be too personal. The image speaks. . . . An attitude means a style. A style means an attitude. Implicit in our attitude is a belief in freedom . . ." reads his first program note in 1956, and in 1957 the tone is the same: "This program is not put before you as an achievement, but as an aim. We ask you to view it not as critics, not as a diversion, but in direct relation to a British cinema still obstinately class-bound; still rejecting the stimulus of contemporary life, as well as the responsibility to criticise; still reflecting a metropolitan Southern English culture which excludes the rich diversity of tradition and personality which is the whole of Britain."[30]

How similar it all sounds to his first major critical article ("Angles of Approach") in 1947, which he began by proclaiming, "There has been no revolution. Most people still demand nothing more from the cinema than that it should provide them with light entertainment" and went on to condemn "middle-brow" attitudes to art: "From the cinema the low-brow demands diversion, nothing more. The middle-brow, however, is on the highroad to art and culture. He is aware, just, of what we may call fundamentals, and he thinks that a good film should show itself aware of them, too. But he is incapacitated by a dislike of reality—reality plain, that is; what he likes, what he rapturously accepts, is reality romanticised."[31] For an initial critical effort, the essay is impressive, primarily for that authoritarian tone which would become Anderson's trademark in both print and film, a tone which combines abruptness, concision, contempt for the obvious, and absolute disregard for sacred conventions—qualities rare enough in a culture where other critics could offer such 'insights' as, "I have never understood the taste for violence and squalor in the cinema. We know that dreadful things go on all around us; we know that life is grim and we deplore it; but I can see no merit in bringing the misery into our recreation," or could warn others to stay away from all that "technical mumbo-jumbo" and "eat the pudding, not meddle in the kitchen."[32] (Such squeamish rhetoric did not fade away in the sixties; a *Commonweal* reviewer of *This Sporting Life* found the film "too violent for my tastes," the final scenes "downbeat," and the view of the city "on the grubby side."[33])

Regardless of Anderson's view that "the remnants of my critical and polemical past which still survive in people's memories often prove rather embarrassing,"[34] if ever a nation needed a voice geared, as Alexander Walker has said, "to wake up the dull boys in the class,"[35] it was England, and if there ever has been a testament to energy and fortitude in the face of complacence, it is Anderson. All through the late forties and fifties he snapped and barked at the heels of the doughty film industry and its placid critics that they had a "duty" to "stand up! stand up!" "get out and push," and "only connect." Through his writing for *Sequence* from 1947 to 1952, he had the freedom to strike out at what he felt was the British critics' main flaw of "not taking things too seriously,"[36] and thereby contributing to "the proud affirmation of the value of ignorance."[37] If *Cahiers du Cinema* had problems, at least, Anderson felt, it encouraged originality and freshness in filmmaking, for "compared with the French we have the air of a nation of amateurs, in film criticism no less than in any other cultural activity."[38] "It was one of those vitriolic little magazines," Anderson said of *Sequence* in 1973, "people run when they are young. Nobody gets paid, but they have complete charge of things."[39] Though the journal folded in 1952, Gavin Lambert recalls that it "was launched like a firework, expected to light up the sky and then disappear. However, it aroused enough admiration and rage for us to continue . . . for both of us it turned out to be an interlude of self-discovery." The strength of *Sequence*, he feels, lay not in an attempt to create a theoretical base, but in its enthusiasm for good films: "All we basically knew was that we cared about personal films, not official ideas of 'art,' and *Sequence* was partly a series of love letters to directors we admired, partly a succession of hate-mail against work we despised."[40]

Resounding through all of Anderson's essays of this period, though, is the conviction that people, especially the English, must accept the seriousness and value of film as an art form and that critics must stop treating it as if it were second-rate entertainment, useful merely for diversion or education. "It is the critic's first duty," he wrote, ". . . to perceive the object of a film and to judge its success in achieving that object . . . it means allowing every film to justify itself by its own standards, not by our pre-conceptions."[41] His concern with integration underscores every point, for a vital film industry, he felt, was one which should in some way dissolve class differences and deal with the *real* complexities of life, not those fabricated by a romanticized social structure (in which the aristocracy is "a fine old figure of fun" and "the working class characters are chiefly comic, where they are not villainous" and "make excellent servants, good tradesmen, and first-class soldiers").[42] Similarly, vital films would have to catch up with the rest of the Western renaissance and learn that form and content are not separable: "I find this distinction between form and content somewhat naif. It is the essence of poetry (in any medium) that the thing said cannot be critically distinguished from the way of saying it. Perhaps we see here the pernicious influence of a school of 'Film Appreciation' which analyzes every film according to certain textbook conceptions of technique, and which is as insensitive to meaning as it is to subleties of individual style."[43]

It hardly needs to be stressed how unique it is for a critic who repeatedly demands so much from an art form actually to be able to learn from others' mistakes and successes and create works far superior to many of those he has reviewed. But this is exactly what happened with Anderson. He could criticize Elia Kazan for constructing a "brilliant technical surface" in *On the Waterfront* which evades "essential conclusions" and focuses on Marlon Brando's "potency" to "palm off a number of political assertions, all of them spurious and many of them pernicious";[44] but when he made *This Sporting Life* eight years later he actually made a far more "potent" and cohesive film whose "essential conclusions" are a part of the film's structure. He could incessantly inquire why certain techniques were used (Griffith's camera "is tracking for the first [or second] time in the history of the cinema; but where to? . . . from what to what, and why?";[45] color is "too often used for its own sake, substituting for style instead of being assimilated into it"),[46] but when he began to make movies himself, his forms, again, would be integrated with content. His "Perspectives From Cannes," which appeared yearly in *Sight and Sound* in the fifties, could bemoan the persistent phoniness and the "lack . . . of courage, generosity, readiness to expose and commit oneself"[47] in so many films, yet he would be able to take to Cannes (and win the Grand Prix, in 1969) films which were full of "feeling," "affirmation," and "vitality." Even when he was directing episodes of *Robin Hood* for television, he could see the humor of his "writing severe strictures on de Sica and Zavattini in the evening, while knowing that next day I shall be struggling with a custard pie," yet understand "why a director like Ford makes so many films—and doesn't much care if the critics say a lot of them are bad. He likes making films. He likes being on the floor. A unit is a good thing to be part of." [48]

Politics and Polemics

While Anderson was directing these episodes of *Robin Hood*, he wrote one of his last and most important essays, "Get Out and Push," for that manifesto of British liberalism, *Declaration*. Although he claimed just two years later that the essay contained some "unrealistic Liberal aspiration," [49] its intelligence and wit distinguish it from its companion pieces in the collection (only John Osborne's "They Call it Cricket" is as scathing.) But more important, for all its apparent politicism, its fervor points toward an ultimately individualistic position, since to Anderson no party offers real change. The Conservative party is "proudly blinkered to the last," the Labour movement suffers a "failure of imagination," the liberal spirit is "at the moment . . . a weak-limbed caricature," and Socialism "has yet to present its solution dynamically, to shake of its complexion of inferiority and opposition, to speak with confidence, and from the heart." [50]

Again, that familiar call for new identities and images is heard here, and though he sees culture and politics as intimately related, his actual political position is hard to determine. It is predominantly socialist, but, as he says, "Socialism that cannot express itself in emotional, human, poetic terms is one that will never capture the imagination of the people," and "conversely, artists and intellectuals who despise the people, imagine themselves superior to them, and think it clever to talk about the 'Ad-Mass,' are both cutting themselves off from necessary experience and shirking their responsibilities."

Even in 1979 he said, "I have never actually been a Socialist, and I have always questioned people's use of this word in a flabby, humanitarian sense as simply meaning somebody who wanted to be nice to his fellow men, believed in something called equality, and was against poverty and suffering."[51] What comes through most strongly is the belief that the old England is dead and that the power must be generated to create a new nation in tune with twentieth-century realities. But this conviction has never led Anderson to Marxism, about which he said in 1969, "I grow increasingly skeptical of those kinds of solutions. I don't really see change in terms of an effort towards an attainable good end. I think it's just part of the continual structure to which in fact I can see no end. . . . I come to the conclusion that in the end the artist is on his own. Therefore, to that extent, I would consider myself to have an anarchistic rather than a socialist position. I think that a socialist society is as liable to victimize the artist as any other."[52] But still, as he said in 1979, "Being a political director doesn't at all imply that one is making propaganda for any particular political system. My films are as sceptical as they are affirmative. . . . In other words, I don't think that a tendency to knock down (or to test) ideas or systems makes one unpolitical."[53]

So Anderson's politicism is most aptly described as a humanist social awareness (if such a phrase can still reflect a sincere social conscience), a realization that any artist's work is in some way dependent on the politics which surround it, but that ultimately the artist "is on his own." Anderson learned this in the late fifties, when there was a brief attempt to form a leftist coalition of artists and politicians:

I don't regret having tried to join a New Left because it would have been very nice if the New Left had ever amounted to anything, if there really had been a radical movement we could have joined together in, both as writers, filmmakers and politicians. But it did not take very long for the New Left to degenerate into a new generation of politicians or a new generation of academic theorists. And it did not take very long for us to discover that their interest in the arts was a purely propagandist one. It was only in so far as we made work that seemed to reflect what they thought to be socially acceptable that our work was in any way interesting.[54]

So many myths which bolstered the imperialist mentality were collapsing at the time that Anderson felt it was time to pose ultimate questions: "We have a thousand problems to resolve in this country, but the essential one is this: What kind of Britain do we want? What ideal are we going to set ourselves in our re-ordering of society? What truths do *we* hold to be self-evident?"[55]

Significantly, Anderson did not write much criticism after this, and made no more documentaries (except to help direct and edit *March to Aldermaston* in 1958, a chronicle of a protest march on a nuclear armaments factory). Instead, he set about answering these questions through a series of feature films. Twelve years after writing "Get Out and Push," he told an interviewer, "I think that our ability to change the world is exceedingly limited, although I think it's a good thing to feel that we can or that we should. The idea of changing the world can be interpreted in a very large number of ways. . . . Everything depends on the context within which a film is made . . . on an imaginative level, a film like *This Sporting Life* can change the world."[56]

The Politics of Imagination

It is on this "imaginative level" that Anderson worked out his history of change for the next sixteen years, as political issues became translated more and more into questions of personal responsibility and individual creativity. In David Storey, the author of the novel *This Sporting Life* (1961), Anderson found a temperament equally obsessed with the difficulties of creating harmonious social, sexual, and psychological relationships, and their long collaboration which began with *This Sporting Life* has always centered on this essential problem of trying to connect with the world. As Anderson once wrote about the author, "He labours, often desperately, to balance the ambiguities of our nature, our situation: male and female, tenderness and violence, isolation and love."[57] Like the relationship between Frank Machin and Mrs. Hammond in *This Sporting Life*, the Shaws' marriage in *In Celebration* is an example of Storey's fascination with failed potential (or the reasons why "ambiguities" are *not* balanced). Enacted through economic necessity, sustained despite disillusionment, the marriage so touted by Mr. Shaw is simply an uneasy détente; no sensibilities have harmonized, no capabilities have integrated. Like Machin and Mrs. Hammond, Mr. and Mrs. Shaw refuse to experience each other's lives; unlike the more dramatically doomed couple, however, the Shaws have created progeny who at least attempt to integrate the disparate worlds of their parents (and who, in the process, grapple with the emotional and economic implications of the term "marriage" in ways their parents refuse to do).

The industrial northern city in *This Sporting Life*—like that in *In Celebration*—is hopelessly divided between factory owners and workers, wealthy and poor, men and women, but Machin is just as divided within himself. His physique and class limit him to a life of physical performance, but what he ardently desires is some kind of psychological and emotional fulfillment. He cannot connect sexually or spiritually except by force; he cannot even become more than a physical tool of others. In every way, he lands on the bottom. Anderson's use of flashbacks is so intimately connected with these problems that it in itself reveals one of the major fissures in the film: that between past and present—specifically, the *power* of the past and the futility of trying to escape it when everything in one's environment attempts to preserve it. But flashbacks are used for another reason as well, for they show Machin's attempts to understand his life, to become, in other words, a *thinker*, to develop mental capabilities (what are subjective point of view flashbacks if not glimpses of a character's psychological processes?). Machin fails because he cannot generate meaning in his life, cannot become "whole" (even though this is an almost impossible task in his society), and tries to make someone else—his landlady—responsible for his happiness.

Interestingly, Anderson shot *This Sporting Life* in the Yorkshire city of Wakefield, where he filmed his first nonindustrial documentary, *Wakefield Express*. (Anderson was repeatedly drawn to Yorkshire; even his very first "factory" films were shot there, as well as parts of *O Lucky Man!*, and *The White Bus* was shot in Manchester, recalling Free Cinema's distaste for the "cosmopolitan" South.) *Wakefield Express*, a tribute to the centennial of a newspaper, presents a different view of the area, but the view is different because the emphasis is far more general: people creating a strong sense of community, not drawing sharp divisions between work and play. In his documentaries, as a beginning filmmaker, Anderson explores the ways film "subjects" interact, the ways new audience-actor relationships are always forming in reality, and the ultimate impossibility of being "objective." Integration and harmony are sought out in these films, with the people in Wakefield, the deaf children in *Thursday's Children* (1953), and the Covent Garden market workers in *Every Day Except Christmas* all happily aware of the camera, smiling into it, waving out at the audience. Only in *O Dreamland* is this interplay absent, and this is because the amusement park under scrutiny is so lifeless and unimaginative, the people's aesthetic (and aesthetic in a broad sense) criteria so undemanding, the society which produced the park so fragmented. Passivity is the crime here, that willingness to be led about, dished up mediocrity, all to avoid the responsibility of choosing one's pleasures for oneself. (It is, as well, the major crime of the tourists in *The White Bus*, a film which has so much in common with *O Dreamland*, and certainly of Michael Travis in *O Lucky Man!*)

O Dreamland points out an interesting fact about Anderson's documentaries: they show worlds which are either hopelessly detached from reality or successfully integrated into the flow of life *from the start*; there is no struggle to achieve harmony (although the children in *Thursday's Children* make valiant efforts, they are charming to begin with), nor is there a process of disintegration (and in this respect, *The White Bus* and *The Singing Lesson* have far more in common with the documentary tradition than with the features). Anderson's talent in these early years is obvious, but part of that talent consists of choosing situations congenial to his interests. He could have gone on making documentaries after *Every Day Except Christmas*, but if he had singled out one of the faces in Covent Garden or Wakefield and examined that life with as much care as he did Frank Machin's, would such a film have still ended in smiles and laughs? Probably not, and, given Anderson's temperament, had he not begun work in fiction film, he would have been forced into political statements, for what other direction can documentary go if its maker is truly dedicated to change? And although Anderson still finds documentary "a very beautiful and gratifying form to work in,"[58] the fact that his real (or at least visible) evolution began when he entered the realm of fiction tells us where his belief in change really lies: in art, not politics, in individual freedom, not mass movements.

Revolutionary Rumblings

In the late sixties the term "anarchism" began to appear frequently in interviews with Anderson, and when *If* . . . was released the same year the student riots erupted in Europe and the United States, it was often misunderstood as a call for "Revolution." But Mick Travis's story descends metaphorically from Frank Machin's; in a sense, it is the converse of *This Sporting Life*, for where Machin's working class world is bounded by *physical* limitations, Travis's is just as constricted by *mental* checks. If Machin's struggle centers on developing an *inner* life, Travis's centers on developing connections to the *outside* world, to breaking *out* of a cloistered system which denigrates physical realities (the school being an obvious metaphor for England's privileged class, but there are other associations as well).

The film's structure, like that of *This Sporting Life*, reflects this pattern: color and black and white sequences alternate regularly until the end, when black and white is banished for good. Color is used here to "break out" in the same way that flashbacks are used in the earlier film to "break in." Anderson first used alternating color and black and white in *The White Bus*, but black and white dominates—and ends—this film (and appropriately so, since the story seems to "run down" as every hope of imagination in the town in quashed), while color gloriously signals Travis's partial victory over repression. Integration is again the impetus behind *If . . .*—of body and mind, self and society, aggression and passivity ("A sort of personal myth was being worked out,"[59] Anderson claims)—and to emphasize the point made earlier in the chapter, this is revolutionary, especially in a class-bound society. By the time Anderson made *If . . .* there was no doubt that he was committed to *imaginative* revolution: "You must define what revolution is because you can make a revolution by making a film, just as much as by shooting somebody. Maybe better."[60]

If this revolution's goal is to create new identities and images, it will naturally be more successful if carried out on an imaginative level. According to Anderson's view of anarchy, change begins from within and cannot be imposed from without; it must, in other words, be "connected" to an individual's perceptions of the world: a poetic ideal, to be sure. "I'm an anarchist," he has said. "That's my temperament. No authority is necessary . . . the real sense of responsibility is up to the individual. Anarchism is always regarded by the representatives of entrenched authority as an irresponsible creed. But actually it's quite responsible. Because it is the creed according to which we don't do what we're told. We do what we know to be right."[61] Quite clearly, there is no systematic political theory informing this philosophy; if anything, it is a rather open-ended invitation to the workings of one's fantasy, a call for the end of passivity on every level.

This is where Anderson's interest in Brecht comes into focus—not at the polemical juncture but at the imaginative one, where politics and semantics converge into the thoroughfare of aesthetic pleasure.

"The duty of the artist is, not to interpret, not to propagandize, but to create," Anderson said in 1947, and certainly he has never used Brechtian techniques to proselytize. In fact, his 1978 televised production of Alan Bennett's *The Old Crowd* was attacked on this very basis ("Such piffle," he claims, "makes one despair of criticism").[62] The visit of the Berliner Ensemble to England right after Brecht's death in 1956 was one of those felicitous cultural events, for in a year which saw the British failure in the Suez, the production of *Look Back in Anger*, the first Free Cinema program, and the growing popularity of rock and roll, epic theater was perfectly harmonious with the spirit of the time, and inspired rallying cries for all kinds of ideas (everything from public support for the arts and noncommercial theater to Marxist dramas). In terms of Anderson's work, however, we can see how congenial Brecht's epic aesthetics were to a young filmmaker and theater director determined to create new identities and images. As Brecht himself said, "The radical transformation of the theatre can't be the result of some artistic whim. It has simply to correspond to the whole radical transformation of the mentality of our time."[63] Alienation ("a horrible word, by the way, but I suppose we have to use it")[64] is simply a way to encourage understanding, and here Anderson's passion for integrating thought and feeling meshes with Brecht's emphasis on both understanding and enjoying a work. Alienation techniques, like those of the Chinese theater, are means of calling attention to a work of art *as* a work of art, of calling into question the audience's passivity and detachment, self-reflexive devices which Anderson had used even in his documentaries (where his subjects reveal their awareness of themselves as "actors"). The Brechtian view of identity as "infinitely mutable, dependent on particular social and economic circumstances,"[65] the dissolution of easy identification (either of actor with his role or audience with actor), and his idea of narrative as a nonlinear process which reaches no definite resolution are all important elements in Anderson's films, especially *O Lucky Man!* and are compatible with his aesthetic views on film and drama.

"It is dreadful to be asked what a film is about," he said after making *This Sporting Life*. "The film is what it is about. . . . The process of making a film, like the process of making any work of art, should be a process of discovery."[66] This statement is as true for his individual films as it is for his canon of films, but as his last original work, *O Lucky Man!* is a paradigm of Anderson's view of discovery—a process, in a way, which recapitulates a process. A number of adjectives could describe it—Brechtian, Zen, quixotic—but primarily it is Anderson's most complex affirmation of life, a work which carries through the revolution which was prefigured in *This Sporting Life*.

One might have thought that there was nowhere to go after *If . . .*; as Thomas More asks in Robert Bolt's *A Man For All Seasons*, "And when the last law was down, and the Devil turned round on you— where would you hide. . . . This country's planted thick with laws from coast to coast—Man's laws, not God's—and if you cut them down . . . d'you really think you could stand upright in the winds that would blow then?"[67] But in *O Lucky Man!* Anderson shows exactly what is left: people, connecting with others, aware of themselves as the creators of their own lives (or "stories"), and accepting of "reality plain."[68] We have here, at long last, full integration—on the personal, social, and aesthetic levels. After being a manual laborer and lackey (like Frank Machin) and a detached student fast on the road to intellectualism, Michael Travis finally becomes both a thinker *and* a worker, and, as a result, an actor and a creator.

The social strata Michael wanders through are, in the end, simply illusory, for there is only one class: his supporting cast of players. As more and more "veils of illusion" (as Anderson calls them) are stripped away, the most significant series of unions occurs: between Michael and the camera, between Michael and "the director" (played by Anderson), and between Malcolm McDowell and Anderson. Subject-object, role-identity, actor-director—these dichotomies all crumble in one "illumination:" Michael's acknowledgment of the camera and realization that *people*, not ideas or systems, create life. There is no alternation here between past and present, color and black and white; there is even very little linearity. What we have instead is circularity—of both narrative and visual form—as "union" becomes the dominant activity in the film. Merleau-Ponty's words best describe this process in the movies as "an expression of surprise at this inherence of self in the world and in others . . . an attempt to make us *see* the bond between subject and world, between subject and others, rather than to *explain* it."[69]

The evolution Anderson works through from the world of sport and body to that of intellect to that of art is one of the most remarkable on film. But this integration of physical, mental, and imaginative qualities is not based on a premeditated philosophical program; on the contrary, its spontaneous, instinctive nature (and Anderson insists over and over that he never "plans" the direction his instincts take

him) reveals an imaginative process intimately in tune with its
medium, consistently aimed at finding that single image which contains everything. After years of admiring the work of John Ford and
Jean Renoir (" 'Look around you,' these directors are saying, 'and
make the most of your world' "),[70] Anderson himself was able to
create an entire history of "looking around" once he got behind a
camera, and to create the film poetry he so elegantly described in
1959: "What do we mean by poetry? We mean intensity, emotional
force, compression of style, that glow of imagination and feeling that
transforms fact into symbol, story into myth."[71]

2

"Self-Delighting Liberty": The Documentaries

A REPORTER makes his rounds in a Yorkshire town, chatting with his neighbors, searching out stories; deaf children learn to talk, and have great fun doing so; market workers gather in a tea shop after working through the night, arranging beautiful displays. The attitudes and experiences so often missing from the lives of Anderson's later fictional characters are here in these early documentaries: animation, communication, involvement, the surprising synthesis of feeling and place. From the viewpoint of a generation of viewers whose idea of documentary is inherently political, these films could seem misleadingly naive. Certainly Anderson's subjects are the products of tradition: the centennial of a Yorkshire newspaper, the efficient management of a school for deaf children, the habits of workers in London's now defunct Covent Garden marketplace—hardly the stuff of sociological strife (although they certainly could be, in different hands). But then, sociological complexity is not the point.

Anderson always used the documentary form to get at something more interesting, more "poetic," than journalistic complexity. While ostensibly about a newspaper, *Wakefield Express* is really concerned with the ways a community relates both within itself and with its neighboring towns; the newspaper is just a convenient excuse to "show Wakefield its own face." Watching a film of children learning to speak could be incredibly boring, or pathetic, depending on the director's attitude. *Thursday's Children* is neither, for again (but with greater intensity than in *Wakefield Express*), *faces* become the story. But in *Thursday's Children* something different happens which foreshadows everything Anderson works toward in his later films. At the end of the film the children all turn to the camera, laugh, and wave gaily—hardly a "journalistic" ending (which today would probably be a freeze-frame of a child struggling to speak). There is nothing pathetic or patronizing here. Communication, that over-

worked and nebulous term, is established between everyone involved in the film—subjects, cameraman, director, and audience.
Similarly, the Covent Garden workers turn to the camera at the end
of *Every Day Except Christmas* and smile out at the audience (the
final image is even a cartoonlike smiling face). These films are all
involved in experiences other than sociological "truth": openness,
the willingness to make contact with others—in fact, the *responsibility* of establishing communication with the rest of the world. The
people here create their own stories.

"When I make a film about Covent Garden market and those
workers and it is idealized, this is actually a part of myself and the way
I look at life, the way that I look at my fellow human beings. I'm trying
to make other people share that way of looking at life. It doesn't mean
that I'm not capable of being cynical or satirical about them, which I
can also be in a different context."[1] To be sure. It's difficult to imagine
a more scathing attack upon passivity than *O Dreamland*. "Dreamland," the amusement park examined in this twelve minute film, is a
wonderland of expired fantasies: unimaginative diversions, sad little
exhibitions, caged animals. If this is England at play, how much
better it must be to work! (And as several critics have pointed out, the
workers of Anderson's other films would probably frequent Dreamland in their off-hours.) Whatever Scottish impulses might be at work
here, it is strange to see Anderson finding such joy and aesthetic
possibilities in places of *work*, yet nothing but rather muted horror in
leisure spots. Is there no *meaningful* play?

And, of course, there is, as we see particularly clearly at the end of
O Lucky Man! and even, to some extent, in *The Singing Lesson*. But
again, the joyous cast dance of the former film comes only *after* the
completion of the film, and the playful songs of the latter are part of
the students' assignments at the music school. But this is the point:
happiness, amusement, and art should not be diversions from the
"rigors" of life but, rather, integral parts of living. Whenever work
and play are radically sundered, people themselves are psychically
fragmented (and we never see a very happy face in *O Dreamland*;
what we mainly see are parts of bodies—rows of bottoms, queues of
shuffling feet, phalanxes of grabbing hands). What hope is there for
people who so divide their world? Most distressing here are the
children, who seem totally exhausted, in obvious contrast to those in
Thursday's Children.

But even at this stage of his career, Anderson's eye for dramatic
situations was unfailing. All through these early films we see scene

after scene of people creating for each other, whether it be a war memorial service or a school performance in Wakefield, a rendering of *Black Sambo* for the deaf children, an animated storytelling in Albert's Cafe at Covent Garden, or even the various torture replications in Dreamland. While in the latter, the audience stands passively, even moronically, watching whatever is placed before it, the other three films find audience and actors repeatedly changing places, perpetually creating new stories and situations. The people—not the issues—create the films. Anderson made other documentaries (his first industrial shorts and several very brief information films for various government agencies) and helped direct a film about a march on a nuclear armament factory (*March to Aldermaston*), but these four major documentaries reveal most clearly the attitudes which would shape his later films.

Attitudes and Approaches

John Grierson's definition of documentary—"the creative treatment of actuality"—should, Anderson wrote in 1954, "suggest an exciting, endlessly intriguing use of the cinema; and yet it must be admitted that the overtones of the term are not immediately attractive."[2] To try to assess his highly personal works in light of a particular school or theory of documentary is difficult, if not futile. Anderson himself once told an interviewer, when asked repeatedly his definition of documentary, "Just talk about films . . . very often when we use these terms, they only give us an opportunity to avoid really discussing the film."[3] We might agree with the wisdom of this and accept his rather general definition (or the closest he has come to a definition) of the form:

There is a clear distinction between the creative and poetic use of invented elements, and documentary at its purest and most poetic is a form in which the elements that you use are the *actual* elements. It is the manipulation of the *actual* world into, as far as I am concerned, a poetic form—and that is documentary. If you invent your characters, invent your situation, then you go on from documentary into a different form.[4]

Certainly, it is far easier to see what Anderson does *not* value in documentary: journalistic facade ("the merits and demerits" of which "include a certain superficiality and a certain emphasis on effect"), the pretence of objectivity ("There is no such thing as objective truth in art"), and the didacticism of the 1930s documentary tradition.

"One instinctively chooses the approach that reflects one's nature,"
he has said, "and my nature finds the social relationships of human
beings as important and as significant as their personal relations.
Documentary is certainly a form, I think, that stresses the social
relationships, because the nearer you get to the individual study and
the psychological study, the more you are forced towards a dramatic
effort and an imaginative creation and that takes you away from
actuality, which is in fact the basic material of documentary."[5] But
this should not lead one to expect a Marxist perspective in his
documentaries. Anderson, in fact, had no historical "message" in
mind when he made these films: "The way an artist develops or picks
on a subject and decides what he is going to do to a large extent
depends on his own imaginative development, his development as an
artist, and often that will catch him unawares. . . . I don't sit down
and think, now in the present state of society what should one do. I
just think, here I am living from day to day, there are certain
possibilities, I wonder what would be the best thing to do next."[6] In
other words, he was theoretically as far away from Grierson's "tech-
nological/collectivist"[7] approach to society as can be imagined. The
state has withered away—imaginatively—before Anderson's
documentaries even begin, and faces are the story.

The documentarian Anderson most admired was Humphrey
Jennings, and the personal qualities of Jennings's best works, rather
than social or theoretical ideas, seem to have influenced him the
most: "Not the least among the virtues that distinguish Jennings from
almost all British filmmakers is his respect for personality, his freedom from the inhibitions of class-consciousness, his inability to patro-
nize or merely to use the people in his films. Jennings' people are
ends in themselves."[8] Even *March to Aldermaston* seems—to
Anderson—just as much about the ways people interact as about
nuclear protest. Although some kind of montage or dialectic structure is apparent in *O Dreamland*, what seems to govern the films is a
growing feel for rhythm, for finding a perfect fusion of form and
content. Significantly, *O Dreamland* is the one documentary which is
critical of its subject and which sets up contrasts and comparisons; the
others show no interest in this type of critical form.

Beginner though he was, Anderson approached his subjects from a
unique, nontraditional angle. For example, a typical journalistic
opening to *Wakefield Express* would have been the historical sequence which appears several minutes into the film—starting a film
about a newspaper's centennial, in other words, at the "logical"

place: the history of the town. Another obvious starting point would have been scenes depicting the production of the paper itself, the "from-press-to-people" approach. But all of the technical information about the presses, the typesetters, and the raw paper, makes up one of the final sequences. Where Anderson *does* begin is exactly where his stories always begin: not with background information, but with people. Before we see the reporter making his rounds, though, we encounter another example of Anderson's attempts not only to correlate his structure with his subject matter, but to approach these subjects with good humor, instead of the drab seriousness affected by so many documentaries: to the accompaniment of singing children we see the credits typed out and edited as if they were newsprint. In *Thursday's Children* he tries something different, although that same form/content synthesis is evident: before the images appear, we hear Richard Burton's commentary ("Monday's child is fair of face . . ."); the screen is black until he speaks the line about Thursday's child having "far to go," then we see a deaf child walking away from the camera. The technique, in essence, is at least an attempt to create the same kind of isolation felt by the children. In addition, Burton's eloquence which so dominates the first seconds of the film only accentuates how much the children miss by not being able to speak or hear. "Really, any subject I undertook I always wanted to turn into what I thought would be in some way a work of art," [9] Anderson has said, and this is borne out by the differences between these early documentaries—the fact that in every one he experiments with new approaches and rarely does the same thing twice (except, it should be noted, focus more and more intensely on people's faces).

Interestingly, although these films were made without recording the sound at the time, [10] Anderson resisted the temptation to "hug convention" (as he would call it) and fill the soundtrack with incessant, ponderous commentary. His one criticism of some of Jennings's films was not idle:

Although it is evident that the imagination at work in all these early pictures is instinctively a cinematic one, in none of them does one feel that the imagination is working with absolute freedom. All the films are accompanied by commentaries, in some cases crudely propagandistic, in others serviceable and decent enough; but almost consistently these off-screen words clog and impede the progress of the picture. The images are so justly chosen, and so explicitly assembled, that there is nothing for the commentator to say. The effect . . . is cramped. [11]

Sound, in fact, is quite imaginatively used in the films: children sing all through *Wakefield Express* (as in *If . . .*) and typewriters clack; silence pervades certain scenes in *Thursday's Children*; Frankie Laine howls away in *O Dreamland*; and BBC broadcasts crackle through radios in *Every Day Except Christmas*. Such elements only enhance the feeling that Anderson is really putting together works of art, not newsreels.

The Early Documentaries: Communities of Faces

The emphasis in *Wakefield Express* is not on the paper itself, either as an institution or as some sort of persuasive tool. It is on the people of the West Riding communities and more specifically on the fact that *they* create the stories which appear in the paper. "The point is," the film's commentator says, "that one never knows where a story might be," and it is this randomness which Anderson and cameraman Walter Lassally follow throughout the film, tracking along the roads, moving through houses, stopping to record a memorial service or a celebration. "The odd encounters," in other words, make not only the paper but the film.

So often, however, these odd encounters are miniature dramas of some sort: rugby games, children's shows for parents, commemorative gatherings. And increasingly, Anderson is attracted to just these types of situations, where he can explore the faces and behavior of the audience and the actors; and, characteristically, what so often happens is that the audience becomes far more interesting than the actors, becoming, in effect, the "star" of the films. Even in this first, nonindustrial film, Anderson is not content simply to set up a subject-object study. The paper cannot "examine" the townspeople since it *is* the townspeople; the audience at these gatherings is not composed of dull, passive spectators (as it will be in *The White Bus*) since the celebrations and rituals spring from their own traditions and community spirit. And to extend this reasoning, Anderson cannot be objective about what he is filming, since he is obviously involved: his camera is influencing his "subjects." By the end of *Thursday's Children* he will have given into this idea completely, and the children will ecstatically ham it up for the departing camera.

Anderson wrote admiringly of John Ford in 1955 that "he never goes outside the immediate dramatic context to find his symbols. It is rather a question of intensity within the flow of the drama. Constantly the images are charged with an emotional force so strong that, while continuing to perform a quite straightforward narrative function, they acquire, as it were, a second dimension of existence and meaning: what they are saying becomes inseparable from the way they are saying it." Such intensity is found in the faces of these films as well, faces which, as Anderson further noted about Ford's technique, "carry for that moment the whole weight and intention of the picture."[12] In this respect, the point of *Thursday's Children* is not to show simply the mechanics of learning to speak—a pamphlet could do that—nor to provide biographical or medical data on the children: it is to show people breaking into communication. As in *Wakefield Express*, history and technical information are secondary to understanding. It is the immediate situation and the people before the camera which are important. Paradoxically, for all the emphasis the commentary places on speech problems, the real point of the film is expressed near the end: "Faces are brighter when there is understanding in them. Eyes and hands are lively, expressing what words cannot say." That these lively, happy children seem to be communicating brilliantly with each other and with the camera removes any trace of pity from the film; such respect is what finally makes the film admirable and what saves it from what Anderson saw as some of the worst aspects of lazy Neorealism: "The faintest suspicion of patronage . . . a fatal detachment . . . between director and material, an attitude nearer to indulgent patronage than to love. . . ."[13]

O Dreamland: Trivial Pleasures, Paralyzed Imagination

Given such an attitude, it may seem ironic that Anderson's next project was *O Dreamland*, an admittedly "rather satirical and fairly harsh kind of human comment"[14] on an amusement park he noticed in Margate while filming *Thursday's Children*. (One need only imagine how someone like Fellini would have viewed the park to see how truly "harsh" Anderson's treatment is.) The irony is inherent in the disparity between the two subjects, not in Anderson's perception, for the children who seem to have so much going against them are actually living imaginative, vital lives, while several miles away a surge of "undeprived," fully sensate people are trudging through a severed world of deteriorated fantasy.

These park patrons are a great deal like the "moronic mass audience"[15] who, Anderson noted in 1948, spend their Sunday evenings queuing in front of bad movies. In fact, the Joubert "pensee" he once applied to a prosaic film history exhibit could just as easily apply

to Dreamland: "Nothing shrivels up man so much as trivial pleasure." The people's willingness (but such a *dreary* willingness) to
accept the clichés which pass before them condemns them, not
simply the fact that they are *at* the park. Dreamlands, in fact, can only
exist in environments which do not value imagination, and which, in
effect, relegate all enticements to fantasy to the outskirts of town (and
this fact creates a strong association with *If* . . . , in which we find
fantasy again banished beyond the town limits—at the Packhorse
Cafe). If the "dreams" portrayed here are any indication of the
society's imaginative life, how abysmally dull must its "working" life
be? Again, that is exactly the point: if the best people can create for
themselves is an uneasy alliance of interests, if they so rigidly deline-
ate the times and places for "work" and "play," they are indeed
"shriveled up," spending their lives in dreary work and dull play.

The first image of *O Dreamland*, a servant polishing a Bentley to
the tune of "Two Glasses and Hot Toddies," suggests the stasis which
follows. No one gets in the car; in fact, we never see it again, for this
scene cuts to a shot of Dreamland's entrance (seen through a fence)
and people approaching it. The film's major themes are beautifully
imaged in just two scenes: immobility (the car is never driven, but
sits gleaming like a museum piece) and imprisonment (the subtle
appearance of the fence in the second scene presages the multitude of
cages, enclosures, and bars which fill the park).

The first exhibits we see are animated reenactments of executions
(the Rosenbergs and Joan of Arc) and various tortures (such as "Death
By a Thousand Cuts"). Shots of the dummies performing the acts are
intercut with shots of the spectators looking at the shows through
bars; not only are the spectators (by implication) imprisoned by their
absolute fascination with mechanical, repetitious violence, but they
are actually replaced by dummies at the end of the scene (just as the
tourists are in *The White Bus*). Not surprisingly, the dummies exhibit
more signs of life than their human counterparts, waving their arms
and jumping about.

Repressed imagination manifests itself as an obsession with death
and mutilation in the cruelty of the dummy shows. The divorce of
fantasy from "real life," so apparent in the dreary dress and behavior
of the crowd, is absolutely deathly, and the spectators' willingness to
accept as entertainment an endless succession of repetitious gadgets
(from the dummies who perform the same motion over and over to
rows of game machines and circular rides) is a clear indication that
they lack originality. To emphasize this "spiritual mutilation,"

Anderson rarely photographs *whole* bodies; he fills his movie instead
with shots of heads, derrieres, feet, and hands. Only children appear
intact, but defeated and lifeless, a far cry from the children in
Thursday's Children.

Recorded laughter cackles across the soundtrack of several scenes
and seems to emanate from various dummies, so decidedly unjoyous
that its mechanical repetitiveness eventually seems eerily menacing.
Complementing this "hilarity" is a series of shots of the spectators'
faces; none of the exhibitions creates surprise, happiness, or excitement, for the faces register the same expression throughout the film:
blankness, even, at times, the "typical, unimaginative, phlegmatic
smugness of the British working class"[16] which Anderson noticed in
several shots of *March to Aldermaston* (and which should dispel any
notion that Anderson romanticizes the working classes). A huge,
devillike head erected on the side of a building parallels the collective
face of the crowd and, by its appearance during a popular song of the
period, seems to mock the desperate lyrics ("Kiss me, thrill me").

Caged animals provide the only sign of life in the park, nervously
pacing about, obviously eager to escape. As Anderson makes clear by
photographing the people from behind bars and fences, it is *they* who
are imprisoned, for the animals are at least uneasy about their confinement (although a few have apparently given up and turned their
backs to the crowd). The pathos of these images (exaggerated by the
ironic use of Frankie Laine's "I Believe," with its sentimental expressions of charity and goodness) only underscores the bankruptcy
of imagination in people who will accept *caged life* as entertainment,
and mirrors their own "chained-up" existence. The clichés which
adorn the mass-produced hats and dolls sold in booths ("Too young to
be in love," "Drunk again," "To the sweetest girl I know") offer
further testimony to the spectators' lack of imagination.

Juxtaposed with shots of machines such as "The Little Stockbro-
ker," which promise wonderful prizes yet yield junk, are shots of
barkers desperately attempting to sell games and gadgets. The sequence extends Anderson's attack on listless consumers who have no
reaction to what is proffered them, even when they are repeatedly
cheated. The bingo game, in fact, sounds remarkably like a church
service, with the players chanting the numbers along with the caller,
and suggests the authoritarian nature of the park's entertainment.
That popular entertainment can succeed by dint of people's reluc-
tance to be stimulated (and willingness to play unchallenging games
of "follow the leader") is unquestionably implied here.

The last sequence (in the "Magic Garden") is the final ironic comment on the deadening nature of a world divided into "real" and "fantastic" happenings. As the glowing showpiece of the park, the Magic Garden is an incredibly dismal collection of dummies and statues. Although "Sleeping Beauty" is kissed by "Prince Charming," she does not awaken; several imitation Roman statues are spotlighted, but only one person in the crowd looks at them (the rest of the spectators file by like cattle). The Rip Van Winkle character who points at the exhibits and "says" (in a caption), "The dreams I dream are yours to see over there in reality," seems to speak for Anderson, for the "fantasies" in the Magic Garden are only reflections of the crowd's emotional and imaginative sterility. Since Anderson believes that fantasy and reality are inextricably intertwined, the Magic Garden is a fitting symbol of fantasy that has been segregated, homogenized, packaged, and, as a consequence, has withered and died. The camera pulls away from Dreamland, seeing it finally from the sky.

Every Day Except Christmas: The Final Paean to Work

While the camera seems to run out of images to film in Dreamland's circus of redundancy, it becomes, in *Every Day Except Christmas* increasingly engrossed in discovering the myriad of individualized, happy faces of the people who work in London's Covent Garden marketplace. In contrast to Dreamland's Magic Garden, Covent Garden is far more "magical," for it contains an ever-changing spectrum of activity, people, and things.

The film is superficially concerned with the lorry drivers and market workers who bring their goods to the Garden and set up shop during the night, but it is more deeply concerned with a tradition of vital activity, "a kind of idealized, poetic, romanticized view of work,"[17] Anderson once said. The workers are not the dismal sleepwalkers of *O Dreamland* but people who are mentally and physically involved in activity that benefits others. *Every Day Except Christmas* was attacked by the traditional documentary makers of the 1930s because, as Anderson recalls, "it didn't have any information about the pay of the porters in Covent Garden market or the frequencies of strikes." There was even pressure to withdraw the film from competition at the Venice Film Festival (where it won the Grand Prix): "There had been representations, I think from the Ambassador . . . to stop the film being shown, because they said it gave a very poor view of British life."[18] But as Anderson's program note for the film explains (in fact, as the film itself makes clear): "It is in the light of my belief in human values that I have endeavored to make this film. . . . I want to make people—ordinary people, not just Top People— feel their dignity and their importance, so that they can act from these principles. Only on such principles can confident and healthy action be based."[19]

But there is more to the film than an idealization of work. It is the *nature* of the work examined which is important, the fact that the film creates a visual rhythm which beautifully complements the essentially artistic work of the porters. These are people who work *through* the night, when others are asleep, creating lovely displays of vegetables, fruit, and flowers, and take pleasure in unpacking and revealing things (rather than caging-up things, in the manner of the Dreamland patrons).

In one of the strangest (but nevertheless interesting) commentaries on the film, Rudolf Arnheim bypasses the whole notion of work-as-a-theme to expound on the "thoroughly cubistic" nature of the subject matter:

A world of boxes and crates, irrationally stacked, among which the sturdy warehousemen precariously survive as remnants of organic shape; and fitted into the rectangular coffins, the flowers and the fruits—the traditional subject matter of still lifes, cubistic and otherwise. Was there in the earlier documentaries of Free Cinema the same fatiguing endlessness, the same noises and milling of the crowds, the rapid turnover of innumerable objects and passers-by, adding up to an even texture of unceasing disorder, cut from the loom of time more or less at random, and thus directly related to the abstract paintings of the Jackson Pollock school?[20]

But there is a decidedly nonabstract dimension to the film, which is movement itself. The first scene of the film presents a contrast to that of *O Dreamland*, for there we see the front of a lorry (recalling the front of the Bentley in the earlier film). This lorry, however, *moves* (a man gets in and drives it to London); in contrast to the static, museumlike quality of the Bentley, the lorry is an active, useful machine. Anderson, in fact, chooses to identify with the lorry driver's point of view, moving his camera into the cab to film the passing countryside. Bodies are not visually mutilated or fragmented like those in *O Dreamland*, but are generally filmed in long shot or close-ups to show both the coordinated physical activity of the workers (as they work together to accomplish certain tasks) and their unique personalities. People are named in this movie (the narrator says good-bye to most of them at the end—"Alice and George and Bill and Sid and Alan . . . "), and although the commentary may seem to generalize about the workers, it only does so to place their work in the context of a large, harmonious operation.

The camera follows the workers through the night and captures their cycles of waking and sleeping, working and resting. These cycles establish the human rhythm of the film and emphasize the health of the people and their enterprise (creating, in effect, a "biorhythm"). Everything about these workers contrasts with the spectators in Dreamland, with their narcoleptic shuffling about and unenthusiastic buying and selling. The commercialism of Covent Garden is quite different from that of Dreamland, for the market workers offer goods that have been carefully selected, hand-tended, and painstakingly displayed. A concern with one's work exists in the market that is missing from Dreamland. Accordingly, the camera does not pull away at the end of the film, but comes to rest on the smiling face of a worker.

A Redefinition of "Avant-Garde"

Given the fact that Anderson's later films incorporate so many Brechtian interests, is there any sense in which these documentaries could be described as "epic?" Probably not, but what is evident is a working *toward* an epic sensibility. The passion to break down barriers of all sorts—social, personal, aesthetic—is uniquely Anderson's, but we cannot overlook the pleasure he takes in showing us his subjects' awareness that they are, in essence, actors, both within their immediate day-to-day dramas and the dramas of the films. The only characters who are not conscious of this are the zombies of *O Dreamland*, who, frankly, are not conscious of much at all.

Using Anderson's terminology, we could call these documentaries "avant-garde," for he once used the term to describe Ford's *Wagonmaster*: "Not as implying an experiment in any new -ism, but in the sense in which it is perhaps more frequently used, of an absolute, self-delighting liberty on the artist's part."[21] And this delight, of course, becomes increasingly evident as we near the culmination of *O Lucky Man!* Anderson's focus will remain, though, on those who actively seek involvement with people, art, and life—and, conversely, on those who abdicate all responsibility for their own vitality—but the focus will grow larger, more powerful. Although his next film

(*This Sporting Life*) comes six years later, there is no mistaking the fact that in Frank Machin Anderson finds the perfect subject: an inarticulate, alienated, yet powerful man who wants nothing more that to break out of his isolated, dismal world and become emotionally connected with others.

3

The Primal Politics of
This Sporting Life

AS EASY as it is to detect the seeds of Anderson's later concerns and motifs in his documentaries, there is little evidence in these early films of the brutal energy which characterizes his first commercial feature-length production, made after a five-year "retirement" from filmmaking (during which he directed a number of plays). For a film conceived in the last years of Free Cinema realism, *This Sporting Life* is an anomaly. If anyone could have rekindled the dying fires of "commitment," it was Anderson, but his effort was not merely resuscitative. That willful (and proud!) alienation from middle-class respectability which had energized Free Cinema seven years earlier became the whole point—as with no other film before it—of *This Sporting Life*. In fact, one could say that Anderson carried through his original philosophical commitment to its logical conclusion: a movie whose unusual power rammed against—and even demolished—the limitations of a movement which had grown predictable and, in some respects, stale. And perhaps it is appropriate that this deceptively "typical" film should appear rather late in the New Wave, for it is, above all, a movie about isolation, lateness, "missed connections."[1]

This Sporting Life has little in common with other ostensibly similar films which preceded it. True, it is a black and white study of lives disfigured by poverty, exploitation, and depressingly lowered expectations; but there is a significant difference. It may be unfair to use *Look Back in Anger* as a touchstone of the "working class" (or "angry") sensibility, since not all of the vital young studs who were beginning to strut about in movies and plays possessed Jimmy Porter's wit and intelligence, but most of them, like Jimmy, had something going for them—whether it was a philosophy of life, a hope, or just lusty vitality. Joe Lampton at least *found* room at the top (in the 1959 film which, as Anderson has pointed out, was hardly a social breakthrough); Albert Finney's Arthur Seaton, a "good time" egotist whose motto was "Don't let the bastards grind you down," found himself a literal stone's throw from middle-class conformity at the end of *Saturday Night and Sunday Morning*; Billy Liar had his fantasies; Tom Curtis lost an eye for a cause in *The Angry Silence*; even Jo, the abandoned waif in *A Taste of Honey*, found the hope of happiness in her pregnancy; and others, like Alan Bates's hero in a *A Kind of Loving*, at least had the luxury of growing disillusioned *through experience* with bourgeois values. All of these characters made connections; they found some degree of security in friends, family, or social conventions. Never, however, in this series of socially "realistic" films had a character been thrust out on the screen with absolutely no resources except his physicality. It is this distinction which so glaringly alienates Richard Harris's Frank Machin from his fictional colleagues: he has nothing. And it is this distinction, of course, which clearly shows Anderson's commitment to the uncommercial, unsentimental, and certainly unbourgeois treatment of human values. There was, he claimed, "no room here for charm or sentimental proletarianism."[2]

Certainly there might have been too much "sentimental proletarianism" by 1963, for the tide of relatively realistic movies in England (beginning in 1959 with *Room at the Top*) had by this time stagnated into a collection of clichés: the obligatory lower-class factory worker beating his head against the barricades of class and tradition to the rhythm of the French New Wave. As Alexander Walker has noted, in one of the more perceptive studies of British films of this period, "Social realism on the screen in Britain had become commercialized and conventionalized: what had been genuinely innovative was now predictable; what had been an individual vision was now an industry formula. . . . 'Glumness,' that perfect onomatopoeic word to express the spiritual deflation of the English, was the characteristic that, when the sheer excitement of revolution had subsided, came to dominate the picture."[3] The unmistakable uniqueness of *This Sporting Life*, however, is its very deviation from this pattern, its acceptance of a certain rawness—not glumness—of reality that is perfectly conveyed by its central metaphor: the rugby match. In a word, it "disturbs." The physical honesty of the film, and especially of the footballer Frank Machin, was a cinematic rarity in its lack of glamour, sentiment, and heroic antics. (And here the comparisons between Brando and Harris fall apart, since Brando's early characters, although primal enough in many respects, lack the fury of frustration and insecurity such brutishness entails and which Harris captures brilliantly.)

This unrefined physicality further distinguishes *This Sporting Life* from the kindred films of its time, for Machin's inability to communicate sets him evolutionary leaps behind the raging, articulate Jimmy Porters of the movement. While not all working class "heroes" were as verbose as Osborne's Porter, most were at least able to give form to their anxieties; in these films, expressiveness was a given, but usually a verbal, not physical, expressiveness. The main characters could be brawny or wiry, they could brawl in the pubs and push each other about, but their bodies were never a story in themselves. Their physiques could *represent* a great deal (pent-up energy, youthful vitality, wasted potential), but it was the rages, the flood of accusations against family or society, the tension-ridden monologues and soliloquies that formed the stuff of New Wave heroism (or rather, antiheroism). For the contrast evoked, it is interesting to remember that the name of David Storey's protagonist in the novel *This Sporting Life* (1960) is *Arthur* Machin, and that by changing the name to *Frank* for the screen, Anderson and Storey were consciously trying to destroy any comparison between their character and the Arthur Seaton of *Saturday Night and Sunday Morning*. Commercial reasons aside, certainly the two characters should have been differentiated, for Seaton understood the rules of his environment far better than Machin. From the beginning of the film, he soliloquizes about his "philosophy" of life; Machin on the other hand, is hardly able to identify so glibly the "bastards" in his society, much less formulate a way to deal with them (and it should be noted that the Machin of the film is quite a bit different from the Machin of the novel, for the latter seems far more attuned to the ironies and injustices around him, if not more intelligent). Anderson's film, in fact, locates an inarticulate, almost preverbal, world in which the main characters' spiritual or psychic desires remain frustrated, uncomprehended, and, except for several anguished gasps of intuition, unspoken. The concern here is not with moving up *or* out, to finding room at either the top or at even a slightly higher level of society; it is with moving *in*, to probing the emotions and ideas which have festered under a brittle scab of repression. While social conditions are partly responsible for much of the characters' misery, they are metaphors as well for more personal, psychological disabilities.

The brutally honest way in which the characters' confusion and isolation are portrayed and the unpatronizing way in which Anderson intuits the nuances of their abysmal loneliness create what is surely the most intense film in the history of British cinema and one of the most passionate films ever produced. As one critic at the time claimed, "It is, simply and naturally, a film of the senses."[4] More to the point, Anderson described it this way: "Throughout *This Sporting Life* we were very aware that we were not making a film about anything representative: we were making a film about something unique. We were not making a film about a 'worker,' but about an extraordinary (and therefore more deeply significant) man, and about an extraordinary relationship. We were not, in a word, making sociology."[5]

Repression and Exhibitionism

For *This Sporting Life* Anderson returned to the north of England (Yorkshire, in fact), but the communal spirit of *Wakefield Express* and even the positive aspects of industrialism found in his earliest documentaries give way here to a bleak landscape of exploitation and hopelessness (which reappeared later when Anderson directed Storey's *In Celebration* for the American Film Theatre). The fictive industrial town of Wakedale is a model of imperialism in which a few "head" figures govern the lives of hundreds of workers in the factories and run the city rugby team, a circumscribed environment which offers no future to a worker who, like Machin, wants to be more than a mere "body."

The movie is in many respects a story of frustrated evolution; it focuses on Machin's attempts to develop an inner life and grow beyond what seems to be his fated role as a physical tool of others. As a man on the brink of self-discovery, Machin appears to hold some promise of breaking out of his divisive world; he is certainly energetic enough and appears to have no family ties to the region. The latter is an important point, for while the Arthur Machin of the novel visits his parents (and even lives with them when his landlady, Mrs. Hammond, orders him to move out), the Frank Machin of the film makes no mention of any relative. Anderson says that the family was omitted from the film for "the usual problems of compression . . . my instinct always being towards a poetic intensity, trying to keep the style charged. Also the problem of keeping the personality of a first-person narration—a very *subjective* tone—without voice-over or anything of that sort. The family was dropped, I think, because it diffused the intensity of the central situation. Too circumstantial. (Prose not poetry)."[6]

Machin's absent family is extremely important for several other reasons as well. Like Mick Travis in both *If . . .* and *O Lucky Man!* Machin possesses no visible blood ties to his environment. None of these three characters so much as mentions a relative, while their acquaintances are surrounded by, or make references to, family (Mrs. Hammond's children; the gathering of relatives at the end of *If . . .* ; the families of Patricia, the vicar, and the released convicts in *O Lucky Man!*). This freedom from parental influence and familial tradition can operate to the characters' advantage, and indeed it does to some degree in *If . . .* and *O Lucky Man!* But it is only a bit in the teeth of Machin's energy, restraining him at every turn from achieving any semblance of independence, aggravating his loneliness. He is not only an emotional orphan, afraid or unable to face life without the insulating security of some sort of authority, but a social orphan as well, a product of centuries of habit and economic expedience, raised with a single function to perform, then abandoned when others perform more efficiently than he. Disinherited, alienated, ultimately replaceable, Machin is steered toward tragedy from the start. As for blame, the film quite clearly shows that emotional and social bondage only feed on each other, for as Anderson says, "No emotional situations can be completely abstracted from their social context."[7]

Social restrictions rein in many of Machin's more liberating impulses, but it is Machin himself who tightens his insecurities into the choking collar of failure. His self-conscious awareness of his intellectual shortcomings leads him to smother his burgeoning consciousness under the soggy blanket of Wakedale's decayed values. Never a bedfellow of the "inner circle," though, he is simply used as a pawn, a prized stud, in their power ploys. More importantly, his relationship with Mrs. Hammond, which forms the focus of the film, is fueled by an irreconcilable clash of temperaments: Machin, the aggressive exhibitionist, berates the repressed woman to be as extroverted and physical as he. Of the differences between the two, Anderson wrote, "Mrs. Hammond . . . is a woman whose feelings, though fierce, are almost continually suppressed. . . . It called for an actress of exceptional 'interior' quality, with real wildness within, as well as the capacity for an iron restraint, qualities Rachel Roberts conveyed brilliantly on the screen. . . . The central character Frank Machin was immensely striking, with an ambiguity of nature, half overbearing, half acutely sensitive."[8]

Their doomed relationship is an almost archetypal battle between the physical and the spiritual, the body and the mind. Each character possesses a dimension more highly developed than that of the other,

The focal relationship in This Sporting Life: *(top) Rachel Roberts as Mrs. Hammond, the landlady, and Richard Harris as Frank Machin; (bottom) Machin faces the symbol of their failure.*

yet they refuse either to complement each other (and thus become "whole" through union) or to strengthen their own underdeveloped dimensions (and become independent). Mrs. Hammond's life-denying involvement with a rather perverse "spirituality" is, poetically, the cause of her death; quite simply, she chooses not to be a physical being. In the novel, Machin describes his landlady as virtually shrinking away: "She didn't want to be seen. Her life, while I'd known her, had been taken up with making herself as small, as negligible as possible. So small that she didn't exist. That was her aim. And it was exactly opposite to mine. It was mainly this I resented. I wanted the real Mrs. Hammond to come popping out. . . ."[9]

This passage is the most concise statement of Machin's orientation toward exteriors, displays, *bigness*. Yet his own shapeless inner life depends on Mrs. Hammond's avowals of love; by expecting her to provide his life with meaning, he denies his own capacity for inner growth and fails to evolve into an independent, "thinking" man. Again, from the novel,

> She had the one hold over me because she knew *I* needed *her* to make me feel whole and wanted. . . . I wanted to have something there for good: I wasn't going to be a footballer for ever. But I was an ape. Big awe-inspiring, something interesting to see perform. No feelings. It'd always helped to have no feelings. So I had no feelings. I was paid not to have feelings. It paid me to have none.[10]

In this respect, the film is faithful to the novel, for as Storey describes his literary ambitions,

> I . . . conceived a sequence of four novels which would constitute a sort of campaign for reintegrating myself. In the first I tried to isolate and come to terms with the physical side in the footballer Machin. In *Flight Into Camden* I isolated the other half, the spiritual, interior, and—as I conceived it—feminine part of my nature by writing a first-person narrative in which the narrator is a woman.[11]

In "coming to terms with the physical side," the movie never relinquishes its obsession with brutality, physical survival, and inevitable failure. It begins and ends in darkness, and even the first image of the narration is one of separation: a yard line on a rugby field which divides the frame into two areas and sets up the controlling metaphor of the film. Storey has said, in reference to his own experience as a professional footballer, that rugby "is a sport played by puritans, not hedonists,"[12] a game so violent that only the crowd is sated by it. The film certainly supports this assessment, portraying rugby as more a test of survival than agility. Played without the protective padding of American football, its combatants limited to delineated territories, the game is, quite simply, a spectacle of pulverization.

Machin finds no emotional satisfaction in this weekly grind; if anything, he is even *more* limited than he was as a miner, for the people around him respond only to his showcased girth and power. As an almost purely physical creature during the first half of the film, a "great ape" or "big cat" to others, even a "big lion with a big appetite" to himself, Machin flaunts a body which is in complete contrast to those of his older patrons. Their physical deformities (Slomer's limp) and attenuation (Weaver's langorous, effeminate form) render them unfit for anything except committee room chat. In fact, Mrs. Weaver, the team owner's wife, must look outside her marriage—to Machin and others— for sexual gratification, finding in Machin the "bigness" of fame and physique so direly lacking in those of her class.

Even off the field, Machin's life is limited to a gridiron of bleak options. Since he lacks intellectual or imaginative power, he can work only in the mines or on the rugby field, two choices immediately established in the film's first flashback. The Wakedale townsmen are, in essence, divided into teams: the debilitated heads (factory and team owners) and the Herculean bodies. No one in the film is both a controller and a worker; no one—except Machin—even attempts such a transition. Consequently, he carries the violent battle of rugby off the field and into every aspect of his life. He wants to grow beyond his physical limitations, to be something more than the "Tarzan"of the football field, but his boast that he has "the guts to stand up and walk about" (certainly the boast of someone who feels trapped in a Neanderthal role) is both metaphorically and literally tenuous. In fact, he has great difficulty walking without help for the first part of the movie and, as he is reminded constantly by his patrons, only stays on the team because of their support. Machin's climb from what Anderson would call the "shadowy and remote world of toil"[13] of the coal mine is painfully slow and arduous, fraught with backslidings and falls. This up-and-down motion ends in failure; the film's last images find him falling first to Mrs. Hammond's floor (after hanging apelike from the rafters) and then, in the last scene, to the rugby field, barely able to get up again, defeated in his desire to evolve into an independent, "standing" man.

Perhaps one reason for Machin's defeat is the form his war against boundaries takes: he literally "breaks in" to anything closed to him. Again, like the rugby field, Machin's world is delineated by innumerable boundaries, both visible and invisible. Whether it is a nightclub, a bedroom, a rugby huddle, or Mrs. Hammond's privacy, Machin's fear of exclusion foments constant invasions. His contempt for—and fear of—barriers, however, masks a tormenting need to define himself by those territories he invades, to appropriate external value systems and become like those he fears.

This "breaking in" is evident even in the structure of the first two thirds of the movie, in which Machin's memories sporadically break into his conscious dealings with others; in fact, nearly every flashback sequence begins with an image of Machin breaking into something. Overlapping dialogue extends this subconscious invasion, as Machin sits immobilized and anaesthetized (by pain and the dentist's ether), defenseless to the workings of his subconscious. This flashback technique, however, is more than a device for summarizing Machin's past. As the scenes cut back and forth from images of Machin's growing self-awareness in the first four flashbacks (in which he moves from being a mute coal miner to seeking verbal communication with Mrs. Hammond) to images of Machin's "present" condition (which moves from mobility to incapacitation), they impede any sense of progress, for we are repeatedly reminded of his ultimate deterioration. The technique suggests that Machin's fate results from his inability to *break out* of situations that immobilize him and weaken his independence. Always moving—in the past— he now has nowhere to go, except deeper into his memories.

The Reversal

The film begins with a literal and figurative fall: not only is Machin punched out during a game, a blow which knocks out some teeth and disables him for the rest of the night, but his hitherto uninterrupted march to rugby stardom has been halted. With his front teeth missing, he is no longer attractive to women (both Mrs. Weaver and Mrs. Hammond tell him his looks are "spoiled"), and, knocked out of the game, he is useless to his team. As a physical hero he is, essentially, dead. It seems we have encountered Machin at a turning point in his life, as his exchange with Slomer later in the film indicates:

MR. SLOMER: You've had a good season.
MACHIN: Until today . . . until today.

After Machin falls to the ground in this opening scene, the first
flashback appears: a brief image of Machin as a coal miner, chewing
gum and drilling into the wall of a dark shaft. From this we cut back to
his attempts to walk off the field; his trainers help him lie down and
then pick him up. Another flashback at this point finds Machin
walking down Mrs. Hammond's staircase, seeing her with her children and dead husband's boots, and leaving the room. Back to the
game again, Machin is now lying on a cot in the locker room, unable
to speak coherently or to move. This rising-and-falling pattern continues throughout the film as Machin recalls his rise from the sub-
terranean blackness of the mines to walk about as big as a hero on the
rugby field. His resentment of Eric Hammond's boots, which his
widow keeps polished by the hearth, reveals his preoccupation with
standing and walking; the boots themselves foreshadow Machin's
ultimate inability to stand and move independently as they sit, empty
and useless, with no one to fill them.
   During the first locker room scene, as a trainer tells Machin, "At
least now you won't be able to shoot your mouth off like you used to,"
two flashbacks find Machin telling Mrs. Hammond, "Can't I talk to
you once as a person? . . . I've been thinking. I'd like to go for a walk.
. . . I like to talk to someone when I'm walking." He seems consciously interested in *being human*, in simply walking and talking,
but he is rebuffed by Mrs. Hammond, who snaps, "I don't need you
pushing in." Machin runs out the door—his typical response to such a
situation. While he can forcibly break through barriers (that *is* his job
as a rugby player, after all), he cannot deal with the ensuing confrontations. Consequently, many confrontations end with his throwing objects, hitting people, and slamming doors behind him.
   The flashbacks continue when Machin is taken to the dentist's
office, and here the "probing" theme (suggested initially by the
mining scene) is fully realized. Under anaesthetic, Machin uncovers
layer after layer of memories; simultaneously, the dentist extracts the
roots of Machin's broken teeth. Ironically, while Machin's memories
center on his attempts to be more than an athlete, to verbalize ideas
and control his environment, the operation temporarily destroys his
capacity for speech. The sequence, then, offers a synopsis of
Machin's tragedy: awakened to the possibility of growing mentally
and thus becoming a fully developed person, Machin must look

outside himself (ultimately to Mrs. Hammond) for the words and ideas he cannot generate.

The Past: Breaking In, Physical Success

The first flashback of the sequence at the dentist's begins with an image of Machin, in his preteam days, standing outside the locked doors of a dancing club. He is once again an outsider; the club guard will admit neither him nor the other gate-crashers because they are either improperly dressed or do not have reservations. Whatever the reason, the club is basically another territory which bars Machin's entrance, an organization which achieves status through its exclusiveness. The rugby team, however, is granted immediate entrance, breaking past Machin and the others, a fact which contributes to Machin's subsequent desire to join the team. To this end, he uses Mr. Johnson, the team's old tag-along, as a virtual wedge, pushing past the guard when he opens the door for Johnson, then later asking Johnson to get him a trial with the team.

Machin continues to break into or past groups of people when he enters the club. His resentment of the spotlighted team (whose captains present trophies on stage to the winning dance team) climaxes in his cutting in on a dancing couple. This is interpreted as a direct challenge to the man, one of the star players, and he and Machin go outside to settle the matter. Without apparent provocation or warning, though, Machin punches two men and attempts to strike a third until he is stopped by having his arms restrained by a group of onlookers. When one of the men asks Machin, "What's all this about?" Machin simply runs away into the shadows of the street.

Besides the obvious dramatic intensity here, one of the most interesting aspects of this sequence is its precise, carefully arranged choreography, for the physical rhythm of the editing, with its abrupt flashbacks and jarring, discordant soundtrack, is perfectly complemented by Machin's inconsistent behavior (and this tension is apparent even in the credit sequence, where the almost eerie music alternates with the roar of a crowd, seeming particularly unsettling since we see nothing but the credits). Much of the time he uses his fists to strike out at whatever excludes him, yet he just as often acts extremely withdrawn and wraps his arms around himself—hugs himself, in fact. In the dancing club, for example, without a word of dialogue, Richard Harris transforms Machin into a petulant loser as he adamantly hugs his hands under his arms while the rest of the audience applauds the winning dance team. In a later scene he strikes a similar pose to signify Machin's unease and self-consciousness in the company of women and when singing on stage. The alternating rhythm of reaching out and withdrawing, working with the rising and falling, breaking in and running away patterns, illustrates Machin's absolute confusion about his relationships with others. He will initiate some sort of overture (for even his violence is a form of awareness), only to find himself unable to respond except in terms of destruction. The nervous restraining of his hands further implies his awakening self-consciousness, for whenever he realizes that he is the object of others' attention (except on the rugby field, the only place he feels at home), he retreats to this childish pose (a pose which, incidentally, foreshadows the fetal position he sleeps in near the end of the film). The dentist tells Machin to "keep your hands in your pockets and you'll feel nothing," but ironically it is this physical withdrawal which stimulates inner growth, since in this pose he recalls a great deal of his past.

Machin's inability to account for his actions worsens throughout the film. People repeatedly ask him his opinions and question his motives; nearly every time he answers, "I don't know." His growing awareness of life as a process he cannot understand only strengthens his hostility, for, again, people seem always to make statements which confuse him (and Mrs. Hammond asks him over and over, "You don't understand, do you?"). Machin is not simply a stupid man, however, happy in his ignorance, but a man highly tuned to his mental inadequacies and frustrated by them—he is, in short, an evolving thinker. But he can never resolve the conflict between his body and his mind, between his exterior, performing self and his interior, reflective self, for he ardently desires the attention of others, yet resents their viewing him as simply a physical marvel.

In the next flashback Machin emerges from the street shadows after the fight to approach Johnson and ask for a tryout with the team. When he does not receive a quick answer, he runs back into the shadows (possibly fearing another rejection), followed by the baffled Johnson. Nevertheless, we next see Machin's head bobbing up and down as he limbers up for his trial game. He seems to search the stadium for a glimpse of Mrs. Hammond, but we later learn (in a flashback-within-a-flashback) that she has refused to come to watch him play. This is hardly surprising, for Mrs. Hammond prefers to fill her time with endless drudgery inside her dark, depressing house (an environment in this respect very much like the "shadowy and remote world of toil" Machin should have left behind when he joined the team). Heavily draped and shuttered, fragmented into isolated rooms behind always closed doors, chilly from her refusal to burn an occasional full fire, her house perfectly reflects her own dismal psyche. As even Machin realizes, "She just put up the shutters and stopped living." The widow rarely looks at Machin; she repeatedly turns away from people, having eyes mostly for paranoically detecting the stares of others and keeping a watch on Eric's boots and photographs.

The contrast between landlady and boarder is never more startling than in the visual juxtaposition of Machin's physical domination of the trial game with Mrs. Hammond's vigil over her husband's grave, where she appears at one point in the scene to be nothing more than a shadow. With her chalk-white face and black clothes, she becomes almost spectral as the movie progresses. But she is not the only "phantom" in Wakedale. Eric, of course, is a ghost in the gloomy house; Johnson vanishes from Machin's life—and the screen—for no apparent reason; the Weavers, as pale and ethereal-looking as decadent gods, along with the crippled Slomer, create a rather degenerate, mysterious triumverate; and most strangely of all, Mrs. Hammond's children never manifest the signs of personality natural to children, speaking only in garbled phrases and affecting no one by their presence. The haunted quality of the film increases, of course, with Mrs. Hammond's death and Machin's nightmarish visions.

The scene following the trial game opens with Machin pushing open the door to the team tearoom—another image of breaking in. Although he seems in control of his life at this point (having just played a "blinder"), Weaver's behavior makes it clear that Machin is simply entering another restricted environment. Gliding up behind Machin and Johnson to pay for their drinks, Weaver does not bother to introduce himself, defining himself, in effect, by his money. Ironically, Machin physically mimics this power maneuver by twisting Johnson's arm to force the old man to divulge Weaver's identity. Machin is blind to the connection between Weaver's intellectual manipulation and his own physical attempts to control others, answering "I don't know," when Johnson questions his cruelty. Machin is far more interested in the attention he is reaping from others, for he becomes excited over Weaver's approach ("I'm surprised, him talking to me like that; he must've been impressed") and anxiously scans the paper to find his name in the sports section. He finds it, tears out the article, reads it over and over, and finally sticks it on his bedroom mirror.

The stark contrast between Machin and Mrs. Hammond is apparent again when Machin returns from his victorious game to the dismal house. He is obviously uncomfortable within the confines of the house (or any house, for that matter). He cannot sit still and talk, but must always jump up and down, hungrily pace the floor, look out windows, nervously grab objects, and, most tellingly, hang apelike from ceiling rafters; he seems incapable of refined, "civilized" behavior. Mrs. Hammond, on the other hand, sits motionless, her head turned away from Machin, and delivers a soliloquy about Eric with her back to the camera. Her obsession with her dead husband centers on the sanctity of his name and his continuing status as lord of the house. She objects to Machin's discussion of Eric with Johnson ("It's bringing Eric's name into it I don't like"), yet her memories of Eric are strangely negative: "He used to say he didn't know why he was living. He used to say, 'Why was I ever made alive?' When he talked like that I felt as if I hadn't been proper to him, hadn't made him feel as if he belonged." Apparently she was just as repressed and miserable during her marriage as she is now, something Machin does not realize until it is too late, even when she admits that her happiest days were spent as, of all things, a bombmaker during the war.

While she claims to "have eyes," Mrs. Hammond is blind to a great deal about Machin. Her resentful assessment of him—"You are self-reliant . . . all that cockiness"—misses the point, for Machin is hardly self-reliant. The pictures of boxers and weight lifters he pastes on his walls and mirror (and the pulp novel *Cry Tough* he tries so hard to read) are simply adolescent images of inflated power. While his hostility to barriers is a positive aspect of his desire to overcome limitations, it also shows how desperately he wants to define himself in accordance with others' expectations. His "cockiness" is simply his way of reveling in his physical image. If anything, like an adolescent, he cannot function on the periphery of popularity; he must be "in," on center stage. Even his mannerisms are pubescent (and his constant gum-chewing is thematically interesting in this respect, since as a food which is never assimilated or fully digested, it offers a perfect metaphor of Machin's inability to learn from experience or to assimilate his knowledge of his own past and grow from it). Machin needs acceptance more than anyone else in the film, as his repeated "break-ins" make clear.

His shadow-boxing performance in front of his mirror leads into the committee room scene, in which Machin flaunts his new egotism by demanding a relatively extravagant salary of one thousand pounds as a starter with the team: "I can't change my mind. I feel I'm worth it." As he waits to hear the verdict on his demands, a sportswriter tells him that the negotiations are merely an intellectual version of rugby, "a game for Weaver's benefit." While Machin believes he has won this round by receiving his demanded salary, the patrons view it differently: having been "bought" by the club, Machin is now a member of the Weaver stable. Accordingly, the patrons (especially Weaver) are condescending toward him, laughing at his unsophisticated behavior and instructing him to "read your check—don't spend it all at once." Machin's picture is taken for the newspaper and it captures a rather ironic image of success: surrounded by the cool, vested businessmen, the bruised and shabbily dressed Machin rigidly clasps hands with Weaver and reaches for his check. The irony deepens as Machin is driven home by Weaver in "a bloody Bentley." Not only is his mobility controlled here by the industrialist (as it will be later, when Machin leaves the dentist's office), but his whole future as well. As Weaver tells him, "Well, if you are approached by other teams you know what to say: 'Property of the City.' " That he now tells Machin that Eric Hammond committed suicide at the factory he owns is a fitting omen, for being one of Weaver's workers *is* a form of suicide. A link is established, then, between Machin and Eric—but only a link in the hopeless chain of being which dictates the order of his society. Machin probably senses some of this, for he bluffs Johnson into thinking he has not signed with the team: "I told them what to do with their stinking, filthy money." But his bluff only continues the psychological warfare of the committee room; while Machin once begged Johnson to get him a trial with the team, he is now in control of Johnson, inflicting the same humiliation he felt before achieving success. He calls off the bluff when the old man starts to cry and tries to give Johnson a share of the money, but already he has adopted the ways of his "superiors" by thinking in terms of financial power; he can thank someone only by paying him.

His excitement continues as he enters the house, jumping up and down from his chair, parading his check before Mrs. Hammond. Her initial disbelief (You're a great ape") dissolves into resentment and she tells him, "It's a bit more than I got when my husband died. You didn't have to do anything for it." Machin's anger at her implication points up once more the differences in their world views, for while

Mrs. Hammond has given up happiness and spontaneity in the conviction that "some people have lives made for them," Machin, with his determination to evolve beyond such "fated" limitations, believes that "some people make their own lives." Her perverse refusal to express or accept love is most understandable from the perspective of this exchange, for she believes that she is fated to suffer and that any deviation from this course is simply temporary, a trick. Sooner or later, she feels, her life will resume its familiar deadly tedium. She explains her fears later in the film:

MACHIN:	I want to hear you say it.
MRS. HAMMOND:	Say what?
MACHIN:	Say you have some feeling for me.
MRS. HAMMOND:	I can't . . . you might just want to hear me say it and then leave.

Why Machin refuses to move out of her claustrophobic, tomb-like house and find brighter quarters is an intriguing question; after all, he can easily afford a more pleasant living arrangement now. For all of his talk, he is trapped, and while he only sees his name and the words "One Thousand Pounds" on his check (which he props up beside his bed), the camera zooms in to focus on the illuminated word "Limited" (part of the bank's title). What he does buy with this money is a car. This prized status object, which he shows off to his lower-class neighborhood, affords him a physical way out of the enclosed worlds of team and house and offers at least a respite from the enveloping dreariness of Wakedale. Appropriately, the one time he and Mrs. Hammond leave the city limits they seem free of their usual inhibitions and demands. Although Mrs. Hammond is initially attracted to the ruins of an abbey, she soon turns her back to it and becomes absorbed in the play of Machin and the children, becoming for once a spectator and participant in something besides her dismal chores. This episode constitutes their only attempt to break out, to seek actively a release from their "fated" tedium; the attempt is fruitless, for they return to Wakedale to resume their destructive lives.

The Growth of Self-Consciousness

While, as we see in further flashbacks, Machin always pushed himself into the view of crowds, he now sequesters himself in a bedroom during Weaver's party (which follows, chronologically, the dentist's operation). He is the only player without a date and for the first time does not show off for an audience. He gingerly picks his way among pairs of lovers—even, characteristically, breaking in on a couple in a bedroom—to find an isolated room.

The self-consciousness which develops in the flashbacks he experiences here takes on more overt characteristics: he starts wearing monogrammed shirts, he gladly signs autographs, he proudly lumbers across the field as a crowd cheers him, and, most amazingly, he sings before an audience at a nightclub. But, as his interview with the Weavers after a game makes clear, he is growing only within the limits of a controlled environment. Their comments about him ("Punk kid, isn't he?" "He's not like I pictured") and to him ("My husband keeps his protégés too much to himself"), coupled with their paternalistic condescension toward him (laughing at his unsophisticated remarks with a noblesse-oblige attitude), reveal Machin's position in this world. To his patrons, Machin is simply one of a stable of workhorses, urged by them to "keep up the good work." Mrs. Weaver's attempted seduction of Machin later in the film only reinforces this idea, for she views him as something of a call boy, ready, because of his indentured status to her husband, to service her sexual needs. She even calls him "a big cat . . . always moving," evidence enough of her fascination with his animal-like dimension. Machin may sneer at this comment and refuse to be seduced, but his loyalty to Mr. Weaver (out of either fear or respect) undercuts whatever freedom he achieves here.

In one of the last flashbacks, Machin finds Johnson waiting for him after a particularly successful performance on the field. Brushing past him with a brusque "Hi, Dad," Machin gets into his car and drives off, ignoring the old man he had previously befriended. This is the last time we see Johnson in the film; having used the old man to gain entrance into a world otherwise closed to him, Machin now shuts him out of his life (the metaphor is made especially clear in the number of times Machin literally closes a door on Johnson). Johnson has become Machin's "little dog" (as Weaver calls him), an animal trailing about after his master, the lowest link in the rugby chain of power. He will never be seen again, implying his death both in terms of a world to which he is useless and in terms of Machin's cruelty to him. In the novel, Machin describes him as simply "a withered limb of my ambition."[14] When Machin asks about Johnson, it is too late; the old man has disappeared from his rooming house, a filthy house of horrors in which Machin himself ends up.

Emotional Failure

Of all the possible songs Machin could sing at the nightclub's amateur night, he chooses the most appropriate: "Here in My Heart (I'm Alone and So Lonely)." The all too familiar contrast between his outer and inner "selves" is never more obvious than in this scene, as he stands spotlighted before an audience, singing about spiritual emptiness. Although he is cheered by the crowd as a hero and a good sport, Machin is unable to talk with the women at his table, once more hiding his hands in a posture resembling a self-hug and later embarrassing the women by pounding on the table for drinks.

His relationship with women is particularly problematic, for throughout the movie Mrs. Hammond upbraids Machin for not having "friends your own age," and it is apparent, especially in the nightclub scene, that Machin cannot communicate with women his own age. Except for his friendship with his teammate Maurice, Machin deals exclusively with people older (or seemingly older) than himself: Mrs. Hammond, Slomer, the Weavers, and Johnson. His need for authority figures and estrangement from his contemporaries seem to feed on each other; it is, of course, appropriate that the band which accompanies him in the nightclub is called "The Misfits."

Machin and Mrs. Hammond consummate their relationship, but it is only a brief truce in their continuing war. The failure of physical involvement to sustain their lives—in fact, the failure of sex, by itself, to effect change—is made clear by the destructive process of their consummation. When Machin comes home from the club, he pounds drunkenly on the door ("Get the door open; there's not a bloody war on!") and is barely able to climb the stairs to his room, sliding backward to the floor. Telling the disapproving widow, "You're not my mother. You're something-or-other," Machin asks to be allowed to call her "Sunshine." They retire to separate rooms, but in the morning Machin wrestles her to his bed, physically overpowering her. This is not enough for him, though; he now wants words. Angered when Mrs. Hammond refuses to speak to him after their intimacy ("Aren't you going to say something?"), he hurls his thermos across the room and slams out the door.

As if in retreat from the deep waters of psychological complexity he now finds himself in, Machin runs from Mrs. Hammond to the team tearoom, where he returns to his old exhibitionism, showing off for a group of "old frogs" (patrons and ex-players). By telling tall tales of his exploits on the field and loudly complaining to a sportswriter that "my pictures are getting smaller. Take care of that and give me a little smile when I score," Machin appears to be the supreme egotist, creating and living up to an image of himself as a superjock (although his "shrinking" images in the newspaper indicate his imminent physical deterioration). His mountain of fan mail, including Mrs. Weaver's invitation to "tea," only inflates his boasts, for as he says to Maurice, "She just thinks I'm good-looking. . . . Women, they don't frighten me." All of this bravado, however, dissolves when he actually confronts Mrs. Weaver and her sexual aggression, for while he first tells her, "You see something and you go out and get it—it's as simple as that," it is she who is grabbing. When she kisses him, his first response is to say, "I don't know"; his second, to leave. Although he tries to explain his confusion to her, she refuses to listen, saying simply, "Either come in or go." This statement, which overlaps into images of Machin falling back on the bed at Weaver's party, raises a central issue in Machin's development. Always breaking in and running away, never able to stay in *or* out, Machin is an obviously confused man who feels uncomfortable both outside (and, by extension, as an extrovert) and inside (as an introvert); in short, he is a misfit.

The final flashback focuses on Machin's desperate attempts to make Mrs. Hammond verbalize her feelings, to satisfy his desire to grow intellectually and be a part of the world of ideas. But her self-containment, itself a form of self-love, implies to Machin that he is "buying" sex. Unable to accept a purely physical relationship (i.e., one devoid of abstract conversation), he embarks on a crusade to force Mrs. Hammond to verbalize—even idealize—her feelings, as though he cannot accept as *real* anything which is not intellectualized. His appetite for words (especially those he believes people in love should pronounce) grows until by the end of the film he has made Mrs. Hammond the fountainhead of words which will define his life and give it meaning. The "wounded mouth" motif, then (first his and then Mrs. Hammond's, at the end of the film), illustrates both Machin's inability to conceptualize for himself (for he literally cannot talk now, and can later only with the aid of *false* teeth) and the futility of investing others with the power to define one's life. Appropriately, the flashbacks end with Mrs. Hammond's remark to Machin, "You're so big . . . so stupid; you don't give me a chance," followed by Machin's exhausted fall upon the bed in his room.

At this point in the novel, Machin realizes that "she wasn't going to show her need";[15] similarly, a point of realization is reached at this point in the film, for we cut back to Machin at the party to find him sitting up, staring wide-eyed at the camera, blood trickling from his mouth, mumbling, "My God . . . my God," as if he has suddenly understood something about his life. This marks the end of flashbacks in the film, and indicates, as Machin struggles to get up and leave the party, a pivotal point in his development, a point from which he can grow (instead of falling back into the past).

The potential for such growth seems destroyed, however, when he mistakenly breaks into the Weavers' bedroom and becomes trapped in a discussion of his status on the team. Weaver's proclamation that "I carried that boy," and Machin's astonishment at hearing that he did not make the team on his physical merits alone, but from "all the help" he had, prompts him to realize that he is a pawn in the schemes of others. His future in rugby depends on the wavering fancies of his superiors, for as Slomer tells him, "Weaver thought he had some sort of ownership over you. He doesn't like to see it taken away. You'll be okay as long as I'm there. You understand what I mean?"

Instead of struggling out of this bog of exploitative gamesmanship, Machin falls back into his old aggression, smashing into whatever excludes him in an attempt to "belong." He steals liquor from Weaver's house (instead of simply drinking it inside with the other guests) and yells epithets while the others cheer Weaver as the "jolly good fellow." Later he offends the patrons of an exclusive restaurant with his boorish behavior, in the mistaken belief that his money "is all they're interested in." He flaunts his money by overbetting in card games, paying a neighbor for babysitting Mrs. Hammond's children (when the neighbor is simply performing a kindness), and buying Mrs. Hammond an ostentatious fur coat. Money-consciousness pervades the last half of the film, with Mrs. Hammond agreeing to sleep in Machin's room on Christmas Eve ("But just for Christmas, mind"), as if bestowing a gift, and obstinately clinging to her self-image as a "kept woman" who "looks dirty." Machin, too, views life as a battle between buyers and sellers, those with power and those who pander to it, saying of the head waiter in the restaurant, "You call that a job? Traipsing about like a fifty-year-old tart?" Determined to be a controller, Machin adopts the values of those who have power and brags that he knows "how to handle" people. Even his language reflects his attempts to "ape" his superiors, for by telling Mrs. Hammond that the fur coat "won't bite," he is simply echoing Slomer's remark to Machin that the patrons "won't eat you."

Ironically, he finds that Mrs. Hammond has not discarded Eric's boots as a result of their affair, but has simply stored them in a bureau. Obviously, the boots are a symbol of the widow's refusal to relinquish the past and have faith in the future, but they are, on a more subtle level, a reminder of all that eludes Machin now that he has chosen to imprison himself in a false value system: movement, independent stance, domestic tranquillity. In short, he has regressed, not grown. As he runs home from Weaver's party, he stumbles on a railroad track and falls to the ground. The image of Machin's bloody, debilitated body huddled beside a passing train offers a visual translation of the boot metaphor: unable to rise and walk about, Machin is painfully conscious of his exclusion from progress.

The Breakdown

His new behavior only worsens matters between him and Mrs. Hammond, as their argument at Maurice's wedding makes clear. While everyone else is gathered in front of the church to congratulate the newlyweds, Machin and Mrs. Hammond argue in the cemetery. Machin hits her and tries once more to pummel her into verbalizing her feelings.

MRS. HAMMOND: I could say something.
MACHIN: Say it. I want to hear it all.
MRS. HAMMOND: You don't understand at all.

The battle continues in the next scene, with Machin, in the manner of Weaver, asserting his power as keeper of the house. Mrs. Hammond believes Machin has showered her family with possessions because "you love to feel big . . . you're just a great ape on a football field," and in her preoccupation with "pride," feels she can no longer "hold my head up" in the neighborhood. From this point on, as Machin strafes her with demands to "admit" she needs him, Mrs. Hammond begins literally to die. His stubborn refusal to move away from the house, despite her pleas to "get it through your head that we don't need you," is strange in view of the fact that she makes him feel "clumsy, awkward, big, and stupid . . . like I could crush everything." But his idealization of her, making her the center of his spiritual aspirations, and his desire to define himself through someone else, will not allow him to give up the major illusion of his life. Mrs. Hammond's refusal to confer a benediction of words and ideas on their relationship, reserving her valedictions for the dead, and Machin's failure to awaken her physically ensure the final tragedy. Neither the purely physical nor the purely spiritual life can provide fulfillment to the human need to grow, mature, and change; thus, Machin's body begins to fail as Mrs. Hammond's brain deteriorates. Each debilitates the other; instead of sharing with each other the values each possesses, they produce nothing but destruction and death in their sterile relationship. The explicitness of their violent argument at this point could perhaps seem redundant or, worse, melodramatic. But it is consistent with their temperaments: the greater the repression, in other words, the greater the final explosion. Like the battle in *If . . .* and the lab explosion, torture, napalm wars, and other violent scenes in *O Lucky Man!* Machin's and Mrs. Hammond's "war" finally breaks into physical violence and destroys both combatants in the process.

After Machin destroys Mrs. Hammond's "shrine" (by smashing her pictures of Eric) and she shreds his press notices and photographs, their mutual deterioration begins. He has, in effect, killed the essence of her world (she rightly screams, "You want to kill me! You make me feel like nothing!" when he demystifies Eric by discussing the latter's unhappy life and suicide) and she has obliterated the symbols of his. Machin simply cannot grow beyond the limitations and assessments of his newspaper collage (unlike Mick Travis in *If . . .* , who barricades himself in similar fashion behind a bedroom wall of photographs, but who is also able to create a world outside their limitations). Instead of being a positive breaking out of morbidity, Machin's decision finally to leave Mrs. Hammond's house (prompted by her spitting on him, her last act in the film and one which, more than any other, symbolizes her refusal to speak) ensures his decline. Without her to fill his spiritual void, he cannot confront the simple, overwhelming fact of his loneliness; he, like her, withdraws from the world. In the rooming house, he curls up in a fetal position and dreams about a silent, slow-motion rugby game. This nightmarish vision underscores Machin's own tragic *de*volution, as he and the other players grapple in the mud like indistinguishable prehistoric beasts.

Mrs. Hammond is also visually dying in these last scenes. When Machin leaves her house, he tells her, "That's the last you'll ever see." The next time we see her she is lying in a hospital bed, nearly dead, eyes permanently closed in a final rejection of the physical world. Only her head is visible; the rest of her body is swathed in sheets like a mummy, producing the eerie image of a bodiless head—what she has been, in essence, all along.

The deathbed scene is an interesting culmination of the tensions of the movie. Mrs. Hammond's brain rupture should come as no surprise, for by denying all but her mind and the memories it contains she has created a most unnatural psychological situation. She has made her mind her total being, and it, unsupported and unnourished by the body, simply blows apart (literally, it hemorrhages). Machin's last aggressive act, smashing the spider above Mrs. Hammond's bed against the wall with his fist, seems merely symbolic, a final, futile blow to all that oppresses him. This scene, like the argument scene which precedes it, has been critically attacked by some as overblown or melodramatic. Anderson himself offers the following analysis:

The spider at the end was like the chaplain in the drawer in *If*. . . . It's another element of the poetic rather than the literal. The spider was an element in the novel. It was an important gesture of violence. You could say that at the end, the violence of the man continued, that he could never really learn from his experience, although this indulgence in violence leads him to disaster. It kills the woman. He never gets beyond it. He himself is completely destroyed, desolated.[16]

When Mrs. Hammond dies, all Machin can do is return to her house. He has nowhere else to go, no place of his own, no close friends; most pitiably, he cannot even turn to her children for comfort (or comfort them, for that matter). She, in all of her silent, morbid rejection of life, ironically represented life to him. With her death, Machin dies, in spirit, as well. As he runs wildly through her barren house, calling her name, he finds that his old room has been stripped of its furnishings, even including the mattress, that glaring symbol of their failure. The desolation of the house mirrors the desolation of the man, but, of course, the house was empty all along, peopled only by ghosts, tormented souls, half-people. Collapsing to the floor in one final agonized cry of grief, the once swollen hulk of a man is reduced to a huddled, weeping child. One cannot help being reminded of Zampano in Fellini's *La Strada*, another primarily physical creature (although far coarser) who, like Machin, falls to the ground in a moment of realization and weeps, looking like some prehistoric beast which has washed ashore. Both men fail, in essence, to make the midlife transition necessary for human evolution, a transition Jung describes as the growth from "a state in which man is only a tool of instinctive nature, to another in which he is no longer a tool but himself: a transformation of nature into culture, of instinct into spirit."[17]

The final scene finds Machin back on the rugby field. By using slow-motion here, Anderson exaggerates Machin's physical deterioration, for this is not the same Machin of the fast-paced first scene. He is knocked down twice; the first time he is able to walk sluggishly back to the huddle, the second time he can barely raise his body off the ground. "But I could only stare unbelievingly at my legs which had betrayed me," Machin groans at the end of the novel.[18] As he hobbles into the distance to join the other players, his form becomes indistinguishable. The camera does not follow him; it simply watches him dissolve into a distant mass of players. The image then blacks out into the final credits.

Unlike both Mick at the end of *If* . . . and Michael at the end of *O Lucky Man!*, Machin is not visually differentiated in any way in the final shot, for, having failed both to develop his own capacity for thought and to generate values independent of his limited environment, he conveys only exhausted potential. Machin's tragedy is ultimately his inability to create meaning in his own life, to stop looking to others to define his existence. As Anderson makes clear in later films, wholeness begins with an acceptance of one's self by first rejecting the authority of cultural and intellectual traditions (*If* . . .) and then creating unique, personal expressions (*O Lucky Man!*).

4

The White Bus and *The Singing Lesson:*
Severed Roots and Tenuous Connections

IN THE LAST SHOT of *The White Bus*, a girl sits in a chip shop while the faceless proprietors pull up chairs onto tables. "Come on to bed, love," urges one of them. "Oh, no," his wife answers. "If we don't do Saturday's work till Sunday, we won't do Sunday's work till Monday, we won't do Monday's work till Tuesday, we won't do Tuesday's work till Wednesday, we won't do Wednesday's work till Thursday, we won't do Thursday's work till Friday, we won't do Friday's work till Saturday, and Saturday's work will never be done." The screen blacks out.

It seems the "play world" of *O Dreamland* has found its work counterpart here (if it did not in *This Sporting Life*) in the grim image of impersonal tedium. The disembodied voices of the chip shop owners could just as easily belong to any number of other Anderson characters, from the Dreamland patrons, Mrs. Hammond, or even the Housemaster of *If. . . .* But the situation is not exclusively English ("Really, I think you could make a *White Bus* about *any* place," Anderson told me in April 1980), for a year later he found a similar alienation in Warsaw when he made *The Singing Lesson* (*Raz Dwa Trzy*), although the poignancy of this short film is different from that of *The White Bus*. The urban landscape of Warsaw is fraught with historical malaise, so much so that the people seem particularly ineffectual and unable to connect with each other through sheer fatigue. The Manchester area could, from a different perspective than Anderson's, seem just as melancholy, but Anderson wastes no pity on people who consciously *choose* to live such detached lives. These physically robust characters suffer only from imaginative fatigue and terminal passivity.

The people in *O Dreamland* are not the only ones who scuff about in search of any depressing semblance of entertainment; the tourists of *The White Bus* are just as docile and vacuous, allowing themselves to be herded about their town by the mayor's "See Your City" committee. And yet there is a rather appalling difference here, for the latter are not just being shown sideshow diversions, but their very community! The whole notion of listening to lectures and being guided around streets one has grown up on is so far from the spirit of *Wakefield Express* that the dissimilarity tells the story: while the Wakefield citizens create stories and interact daily to create their community, the people of *The White Bus* are dished up the idea of a community and presented with an image of a "progressive" city—their own city—as if they have nothing at all to do with their environment. If this is not the death of roots, what is?

It is not just familial or communal dissociation which blights the urban image here; there is, as well, that implicit national lesion between North and South. In Shelagh Delaney's story "The White Bus" the main character is a young female novelist returning to her northern hometown from London. Anderson, however, has made her a nameless typist who, in fleeing London, finds her hometown connection even more tenuous than her (implied) new roots in the South. Whatever degree of social or economic mobility existed in the 1950s and 1960s, it seems only to have exacerbated the North-South split. One could take the train South, but one could not return to the unforgiving North—at least not as some "new self"; the weight of the past was too heavy, the cultural disparity too great. Such, at least, was the experience of so many fictional characters of this period (one thinks of Margaret Drabble's heroines), especially the dramatic characters of David Storey (*In Celebration* being one of the most severe examples).

There is a connection between *The White Bus* and *This Sporting Life* in the alienation and lack of community and personal interaction. But it is hard to feel the same intense empathy with the main character of the later movie as we do for Frank Machin; and the tourists are essentially cartoon characters (who, interestingly, seem to have a great deal in common with the American tourists in Jacques Tati's *Playtime*, which appeared a year after *The White Bus*). Frank Machin *wants* to make connections; the tourists (and even the word "tourist" conjures up the perfect image of bourgeois torpor) want someone else to provide connections for them, while they maintain a safe distance from the picturesque images paraded before them. (In this respect, they are most closely allied with Michael Travis in *O Lucky Man!*)

The Warsaw music students in *The Singing Lesson* are different, of course. They are connecting with their environment through their art, but the images of the world outside their classroom (which are intercut with their songs) are so bleak, so joyless, that it seems their efforts create just an oasis of vitality in an urban desert. Is this the most to hope for?

Daytripping Through Life

The bus expedition in *The White Bus* is not intended to be a magical mystery tour of Manchester, but through the eyes of the girl it becomes exactly that, for middle-class conventions and attitudes are viewed as the ultimate "trip," incredibly more bizarre than the rather adolescent lysergic fantasies of the Beatles' 1967 film. What the mayor's committee has elected to show on the tour are sights common to nearly any northern English city of the time: the renovation of bomb sites, the town libraries and galleries, the factories ("The places of our past and present and our heritage," says the hostess, whose manner is strikingly similar to that of Mrs. Naidu in *O Lucky Man!* and Arthur Lowe, as the mayor, is every bit as wicked as he is in his reincarnations as the Wakedale mayor and Zingaran president in the same film). The mayor and the hostess have charted a course right through the heart of bourgeois mediocrity. The *real* uniqueness of the place is seen only by the girl.

From the beginning of the film it seems she is the only person who takes notice of peculiar happenings: a man going wild on a London street while listening to a radio broadcast of a rugby game, then smashing his radio to bits; the eerie procession (to the Lourdes train?) of nuns and an iron lung machine at the hometown station; an open abduction of a woman on a city street. None of these events has an explanation; each just happens, yet according to the mayor, everything in the city is perfectly programmed and easily explained.

The surprising bursts of color (which begin when the girl leaves the station) happen just as spontaneously. Unlike the color–black and white pattern in *If . . .* , the alternating color in *The White Bus* follows no strict rule—other than beginning just before the tour and ending during the final "exhibit" (a mock civil defense rescue). But the color here operates in a really comic way, splashing out at odd moments, disappearing just as unpredictably. It is an almost impish mockery of the mayor's well-planned descriptions of the environ-

A pensive moment and fleeting joy in The White Bus.

ment. Furthermore, sound works the same way; sometimes we hear a rather plaintive tune, sometimes absolute silence—it is all totally unpredictable. But while the last sequence of *If* . . . is filmed in color, the last sequence of *The White Bus* is in black and white, and this is appropriate, for as night approaches and the town shuts down, nothing is left to see except lonely, depressed people behind shabbily curtained windows.

Such loneliness is one of the central aspects of the film (as it is in *This Sporting Life*), the obvious irony being that with all the paeans sung to "community" ("Meet people of the city noted for their friendliness," boasts the hostess), with all the hearty good cheer on the bus, no one ever makes contact with anyone else. Even the sexual overtures are botched and ungenerous: the mayor tries to feel the girl's knee and, toward the end of the film, a boy yells at a girl, "You all want it—you won't get any—not from me!"

The film opens in strange silence as we see several shots of a boy (or girl?) stroking a dove while sitting on a barge on the Thames (shades of Michael Travis in jail seven years later). The camera keeps panning more closely to building windows, and finally reaches the typist, alone in her office after working hours (she seems always to be in places which are closed). The first character is never seen again; who was he (she)? This opening is not part of Shelagh Delaney's story; her story begins with the radio smashing. The strangeness of Anderson's opening sequence only accentuates the pervading sense of isolation and missed connections; London itself seems eerily quiet and deserted. Furthermore, the cleaning people take no notice of the girl in the office. They do not even notice when, in one shot, she dangles from the ceiling. From the beginning, then, the film is obsessed not just with personal unrelatedness but with sensory unrelatedness as well—a world *shut down, closed off,* and certainly fragmented.

Fleeing the office, what does the girl encounter? Only more disconnection (the boy with the radio). An apparent boyfriend follows her along the street and into the train station, talking *at* her the whole time (and she has yet to utter a single word at this point in the film), yelling about class-consciousness and qualities he admires in women (just as the black man will lecture her on "technological change" later on). From the train, she tells him she will write, he sings farewell, but that is it for the boy friend. She sits in a car with a crowd of rowdy rugby fans; they drink and sing, but the screen blacks out as they enter a tunnel, and the next thing we know they are being awakened by a railman's sharp raps on the outside of their windows. The fans leave, and she is alone again (except for the Lourdes procession). After walking around a bit, and witnessing the abduction, she gets on the bus. Where is her family? Has she no friends in the city?

The absurdity of the tour increases with every "exhibit" they pass; they all dutifully use walkie-talkies as they are shepherded through a factory; the mayor—in mayoral regalia—lectures them from the street, standing in front of the bus. Those merits of work which we saw in *Wakefield Express* and *Every Day Except Christmas* are nowhere to be found here; work is now something from which to escape, not in which to take pride (even the typist escapes her job), but escape into what? Even off-hours are debased into "leisure activities," as the mayor proudly points out all the relaxation and refreshment facilities available to the workers. But these are merely socially programmed activities—pottery, quilt-making, third-rate dramatics. Work, play, art are all paraded about as if they were the commercial products of a community, not its backbone (the color shot of a quilt festooned with a gay town scene seems particularly ironic). The city library has emblazoned on its ceiling the quotation which will become *If . . .*'s epigraph ("Learning is the principal thing: / therefore get wisdom: / and with all thy getting / get understanding"), but it is, of course, only artifice.

"Money is the root of all progress," the mace bearer proclaims, and no amount of talk can really dispel the fact that the only "progress" in the town has been superficial, merely a stricter regimentation of classes. The urban bleakness is too readily apparent, especially when contrasted with the wealthy neighborhoods the tourists visit. Brief color shots of people in poses reminiscent of Manet's *Dejeuner sur l'Herbe* and Fragonard appear at this point, rather beautiful glimpses of eighteenth- and nineteenth-century leisure, only to be "shot" off the screen by a hunter, as his gun blast jerks the film back to black and white and fells a bird. No long lunches or graceful play in this park; all art (or hint of aesthetic distinction) has been leveled to undisturbing mediocrity. The girls' school orchestra the tourists visit is awful, the mayor moans about the "disgusting" books in the library, the art gallery seems mostly to house stuffed animals. The tour encounters more and more signs of disconnection: the librarian does not react to the mayor's outburst ("Shall we have tea?" she inquires), the gallery attendant will not tell the tourists the elevator is broken. It is entirely fitting that the last exhibit is the civil defense mock-up. The little drama of burning houses and screaming people is really the end of the tour, in a way, for isn't this what the complacence, smugness, and detachment all add up to: the death of the community? Everything is phony at this point, even the tourists, who are finally transformed into dummies.

As the girl flees this scene and picks her way through the very real urban rubble, the town's loneliness closes in around her. A boy angrily accosts a girl in an alley, behind curtained windows a woman plays piano for herself and an old woman shaves a catatonic old man, and the chip shop owners squabble tiresomely about cleaning up. If there were ever an image of a nation shut down (in every sense), this is it. The girl can do nothing, though, except react. In this sense she is like Michael Travis in *O Lucky Man!*, yet because she does not either adopt the attitudes of those around her, as Michael does, or react violently against them, she is beaten down, seemingly paralyzed, by film's end.

Brechtian Impressions

The images of Warsaw, which Anderson intercut with the songs of the students in *The Singing Lesson*, are even bleaker than those of *The White Bus* (one reason being the documentary appearance of these shots, the sense that Warsaw is "really" rather dismal). Unlike the girl, however, the Warsaw students are doing something, even though their efforts seem to affect the environment only through the film. (Interestingly, Anderson's next film takes place in another school, as if the whole notion of education were assuming major metaphorical importance at this point as a fertile ground for breeding the involvement necessary for revolution.)

The film's epigraph tells us that *The Singing Lesson* is "a sketch-book or poem." It goes on to say that "the words of the songs are not important, only their themes, the images and memories they evoke." Obviously, it is *Anderson's* images which are intercut with the songs—the entire film is a highly personal impression of the students' recital: the clapper board at the beginning only emphasizes the fact that the film, not the objective "recital," is the central experience (as in *O Lucky Man!*). Six songs are performed, each one different in attitude, theme, melody, and rhythm. In some ways, the intercutting of songs and "exterior" images, the counterpointing and contrasting themes, foreshadow a similar, highly Brechtian, intercutting between Alan Price's songs and Michael's experiences in *O Lucky Man!*; but here there is no meeting of the two worlds. Students and city life remain separate, drawn together only through their disjunc-

A performer in The Singing Lesson

tion by Anderson's editing. Contrasted with the students' lively songs, their absolute sincerity and involvement, the city people seem abysmally depressed and detached. Very little emotion of any kind is seen, the dominant images being of expressionless faces in trolley cars, mannequinlike shop women, and exhausted bodies in train stations.

Within the classroom, however, Anderson is searching out those by now familiar dramatic situations in which audience and performers interact and exchange places, the faces of the audience assuming as much importance and interest as those of their fellow students who are performing. In characteristic Anderson style, the teacher finally interrupts a number and shows the students how to perform it, in a comic, speeded-up scene (the first of many instances of "teacher interference" in Anderson's work). His elaborate enthusiasm energizes them all, and the class erupts in happy dancing—an ending incredibly similar to that of *O Lucky Man!* and reminiscent of those smiling faces at the end of *Thursday's Children* and *Every Day Except Christmas*.

But in contrast to these films, we see that the gaiety of *The Singing Lesson* comes from the exclusion of the outside world, for Warsaw trudges right along, oblivious to the students. The final image, in fact, is an obviously weary, expressionless woman walking through the street crowds, clutching a single flower. The students do not pour out of their classroom and embrace their fellow countrymen. But just the fact that they can create *in spite of* the surrounding grimness is a major accomplishment. A year later, though, Mick Travis bursts out of *his* classroom, if not to embrace his world, at least to change it.

5

If . . . : Exploding the "Protocol of Ancient Fatuity"

FIVE YEARS after he directed *If* . . . Anderson told an interviewer, "The only way to be of service as an artist is to find a *metaphor*. There's no use making a film that will be dated in two years. You must find a metaphor *before* the event. *If* . . . survives, while films made after the student riots—films made to cash in on the riots—do not survive."[1] At the time of the film's release, however, there were those who felt that *If* . . . would *not* survive, that it was a trendy, literal-minded study of the contemporary student-Establishment confrontations, a soulmate of *Easy Rider* and *The Strawberry Statement*. American critics of the film insisted on dating it, either by framing it in the rhetorical deadwood of the 1960s or relegating it to a shelf in the musty attic of "British interest" films. That the institution of the British public school was indeed a metaphor for, among other things, the lethal separation of intellect from imagination (and the suppression of the latter) seems to have escaped those caught up in "radical-mania," who chose to see it as only a socially repressive force, an instrument of privilege which, as Evelyn Waugh's Captain Grimes says in *Decline and Fall*, "insures the public school man against starvation. One goes through four or five years of perfect hell at an age when life is bound to be hell anyway, and after that the social system never lets one down."[2]

As far as the criticism of the film's supposed literalness goes, certainly the year Mick Travis blazed off the screen in a burst of gunfire many students were repeating his actions—at least in spirit—in both Europe and the United States. The coinciding of *If* . . .'s release with the 1968 revolts was in some ways unfortunate, for the film became critically bound up with its era and is still occasionally referred to as primarily a reflection of its time or, worse, a period piece. The idea for the script, however, had been conceived in 1958 by John Howlett and David Sherwin, and the original script, entitled

Crusaders, was completed in 1960—a good five or six years before the well-publicized Berkeley melees. During the making of the film, Anderson was surprised when his creation began to seem timely: "While we were filming . . . the photographs in the newspapers suddenly began to look like stills from *If* . . . . It certainly suggests that when we were working on the script about two years ago [in 1966], David Sherwin and I were being, to some extent prophetic."[3] Any attempt seriously to correlate Anderson's characters with radicals of the sixties, however, is misguided on several counts—the first being that Mick and his friends bear little resemblance to such ideologically minded protesters, and the second being that Anderson himself was not particularly interested in the latter: "To the extent that the student radicals of '68 were inspired by political philosophy rather than by generous sentiment, I am not very favourable to their memory."[4]

Even so, one cannot overlook the fact that the movie seemed to pose all kinds of threats to film executives and censors at the time and triggered outrage and concern in misinformed critics who believed that Anderson was cashing in on the "youth revolt." The film, in short, appeared at that congested crossroads of the Anglo-American movie business where both commercialism and art, politics and finance, converged to create one of the most confusing (but nevertheless stimulating) bottlenecks of interests in the history of cinema. The controversy whipped up by *If* . . .'s promotional campaign (posters featuring machine-gun-toting youths with hand grenades above the caption "Which side will you be on?"), not to mention the furor caused by an "incendiary" story line, guaranteed a bonanza at the box office but obscured the most interesting, nonhistorical dimensions of the film in a smokescreen of particularly sixties issues.

If . . .'s impact was indeed revolutionary in the corporate world of film executives. Turned down twice (by Universal and CBS), and even offered to Nicholas Ray (who preferred to see an Englishman direct it), the script landed with Paramount only through the intervention of Albert Finney (whose Memorial Enterprises owned the rights to the script). Even then, the film barely made it to the theaters, for the men in control were disappointed and apprehensive about several aspects of Anderson's direction. First, the executives and distributors were confused by the "reality-fantasy" shifts in the movie—so much so that Paramount's European chief wanted Anderson to "define by music or photography, say, the moments when we go from reality to fantasy."[5] Further, the executives were concerned

about the use of guns in the movie. Appearing in the wake of the
assassinations of Robert Kennedy and Martin Luther King, their
reasoning went, the film might seem to *glorify* guns at a time when
many citizens were appealing for gun *control*. Finally, and least
surprisingly, it was felt that the film might appear to sanction the
campus insurrections which had broken out that year and perhaps
even encourage *more* of them.

Had a handful of people not voiced their confidence in Anderson's
work, the film most certainly would have been put in cold storage for
years, locked up by the very narrow-mindedness it attacks, and one
of England's most original contributions to world cinema would have
been either butchered or buried by the misguided passions of murky
sociology and naive civic-consciousness. As it was, it received an "X"
rating in the United States (forcing the distributors to excise certain
brief shots of nudity) and was met with similar disapproval in other
countries, although finally winning the Golden Palm at Cannes. If we
accept the idea that, as Anderson once remarked, the film confronts
people "with the two things they fear most—birth and death . . .
that's what the film is about,"[6] then the critical wariness toward the
movie becomes more understandable than it would be if we believed
the censors were solely afraid of Mick Travis's pseudo-radical behavior.

In retrospect, it is easy to see that Mick's naiveté is both an
intentional aspect of his characterization and a central element of the
movie. Under a gloss of hardened radical rhetoric stirs an ingenuous
outrage at injustice. Mick's pronouncements are at heart rather
simplistic ("I gave him a line like 'Violence and revolution are the
only pure acts,'" Anderson says, "as a sendup of adolescent intellectual anarchism");[7] his "violent" dorm room decorations look like
harmless paraphernalia collected from the back pages of *Rolling
Stone*. To believe *If . . .* is purely political—in a narrow, propagandistic sense—is to ignore both the other issues it raises and, not least
of all, its uniquely subtle humor.

But even though Mick is hardly representative of sixties' ideo-
logues (he is interested in neither Marxist ideology nor "revolution
for the hell of it"), he shares their fascination with intellectual control.
And even though his "revolution," in Anderson's view, is not complete—after all, he ends up shooting a gun, not a camera—it does
mark a transition from Frank Machin's inability, in *This Sporting
Life*, to transcend his limiting environment: at least Mick blows up
what he hates; Machin is trapped by it (as is the girl in *The White Bus*)

Old Identities, Old Images

The most common assumption about *If* . . . is that it is Anderson's vitriolic revenge on British public schools, an anglicized *400 Blows* which condemns a society for abusing its youth. Anderson certainly has been no *theoretical* friend of public schools; in 1957 he wrote, "Obviously the greatest single factor in keeping England a classbound society is the fact that education is conducted along lines dictated by considerations of class. If you want to move towards a classless society, reorganize education. . . . The public schools remain, as part of a system of rewards. If you are 'successful,' i.e. make money, one of the ways in which your success is rewarded is the power to send your children to expensive schools, where they will receive . . . the unalterable marks of membership of the governing class. Who am I to try to interfere with anything so deep-rooted?"[8] True, Anderson filmed a great deal of *If* . . . on location at his old grammar school, Cheltenham College, but this should not necessarily prompt one to shout, "Aha!" He has claimed countless times that he actually enjoyed school and was not a tormented rebel in search of a cause: "I liked my school. It was a pleasant, friendly place. I wasn't radically critical. . . . I think there's a lot of affection in the film. I was attracted to the subject first of all by the sort of nostalgic feeling most people have for their schooldays."[9]

Such "affectionate nostalgia" has often been misconstrued, however, as a cynical playing around with the myths of school—the contrasting of misty long shots of campus buildings with the horrific repression within the buildings, for example, being an effective debunking of certain idealistic notions of "schooldays." But the affection is really there and runs more deeply than the waspish derision of an "insider." "I couldn't go back to Greek and Latin after the Army,"[10] Anderson said in 1960, which he meant, perhaps, not as a put-down or ridicule of classical education, but as an acknowledgment of just how distinct the worlds of innocence and experience are to someone who has been initiated into overwhelming political, social, and personal realities. And this "far-off" quality is certainly there in *If* . . . , in those long shots, for instance, which appear while faraway boys sing old college hymns.

But Anderson is not just pining away, moist-eyed, for lost youth (a yearning he would no doubt term "unhealthy"), because tempering every perspective in the film is a buoyant, subtle humor. The tone of *If* . . . , in fact, is so much like that of one of his most famous articles

("Get Out and Push") that it could be a visualization of the opening paragraphs:

For coming back to Britain is also, in many respects, like going back to the nursery. The outside world, the dangerous world, is shut away: its sounds are muffled. Cretonne curtains are drawn, with a pretty pattern on them of the Queen and her fairy-tale Prince, riding to Westminster in a golden coach. Nanny lights the fire, and sits herself down with a nice cup of tea and yesterday's *Daily Express*; but she keeps half an eye on us too, as we bring out our trophies from abroad, the books and pictures we have managed to get past the customs. (Nanny has a pair of scissors handy, to cut out anything it wouldn't be right for children to see.) The clock ticks on. The servants are all downstairs, watching T.V. Mummy and Daddy have gone to the new Noel Coward play at the Globe. Sometimes there is a bang from the street outside—a backfire, says Nanny. Sometimes there's a scream from the cellar—Nanny's lips tighten, but she doesn't say anything. . . . Is it to be wondered at that, from time to time, a window is found open, and the family is diminished by one?[11]

Cynical, yes, but the passage is virtually swaddled in good-natured intimacy with its subject. The "nursery" atmosphere of 1957 Britain was recreated ten years later in *If . . .* (that scene of the housemaster singing along with his flute-playing wife in bed while the matron dozes and Mick and his friends plot revolt, for example, is just too much like the unreal complacence of Mummy, Daddy, and Nanny). Like the members of College House's "family," those of Anderson's essay are not evil, but humorously, even pathetically, out of touch. The school world of *If . . .* is really no different from this, for if Anderson had continued his house metaphor, he surely would have discovered the same kinky eccentricities among the members of the family as those that bedevil the school people (kinkiness being one of the more logical, and certainly one of the funniest, responses to claustrophobic repression).

Although *This Sporting Life* has some hilarious moments, its tone is obviously different from that of *If . . .* . Both films share a central metaphor, "the house," but in the earlier film the image is laden with *tragic* dimensions, while in *If . . .* it is—for all its hideous closets— a source of comedy. How this image manages to change so drastically in just two movies is a result of each work's actual and figurative movement. Mrs. Hammond's house is a symbol to Frank Machin of everything he cannot attain: spiritual connections, psychological depth, "roots"—in short, an *inner* life. Always an outsider, he is obsessed with breaking *in*, with crawling closer and closer toward

"*Going back to the nursery*": (top) Anderson takes over for Nanny in If . . . ; (bottom) "a bang" sends Establishment types fleeing the film's concluding holocaust.

some mysterious "core of meaning." Mick is the opposite. He *is* an insider, a member of a privileged class, a prisoner of its suffocating values, whose obsession is with moving *out*—farther and farther away from a "core of meaning" which is most certainly rotten. Recalling Suzanne Langer's point that tragedy deals with the culmination of life while comedy deals with its possibilities, we can see that Machin's mission cannot be humorous. An ideal holds his life together; without it, he is nothing. Mick, however, is more concerned with throwing over, or belittling, an ideal; without *it*, he is everything.

The ways these characters view themselves physically tell even more about their divergent courses. Machin models his behavior on a certain ideal of masculinity, the animal/athlete, which is perfectly in harmony with the class system of his society. The photographs of weight lifters and boxers on his mirror only intensify this fantasy image. When he realizes his limitations, though, he has nothing to fall back on; he simply cannot generate a new self-image and is trapped on the lined field, caged like a defeated animal in a delapidated zoo. Mick and his friends are more fortunate. They try on and discard a variety of social cloaks before deciding on the one which will distance them the most from their environment: the urban guerrilla, an image which could never be dreamed by their teachers, families, or chaplains. (Stretching the point a bit, perhaps, one might be impressed by the evolution here in the definition of the term "guerrilla," from animal-man—Machin's apish or "gorilla"-like demeanor—to thinking-man.)

Most of the boys in *If . . .* , in fact, are obsessed with self-images, and it is no wonder, for denied any recognition of their own imagination, they are left little recourse except to become narcissistic in order to salvage some sense of self. It seems their sole function is to serve as targets for the psychological projections of teachers and social class—to be reformed in the image of pasty sycophants. But such "recreating" of malleable young bodies, which is the administrators' only imaginative release in the film, is really only a cloning operation, a rather efficient method of replicating proper little standard bearers for God and Country. It seems that those critics John Osborne once called "fashionable turnips, death's heads of imagination and feeling" have sprouted to flaccid life a decade later, turning, with their "savage thirst for trimmed-off explanations," the fertile ground of the school into a desert of "deluded pedants."[12]

Sterility, inflexibility, degeneracy—ironically, these are the "life forces" of the institution, the qualities which ensure its protracted senescence. Professor Stewart's brief lecture early in the film on the failure of imagination in nineteenth-century Europe could easily apply to Mick's college:

In studying the nineteenth century, one thing will be clear—that the growth of technology, telegraph, cheap newspapers, railways, transport—is matched by a failure of imagination . . . a fatal inability to understand the meaning and consequences of all those levers and wires and railways. Climaxing in 1914 when the German Kaiser is told by his generals that he cannot stop the war he has started because it would spoil the railway timetables upon which victory depended.

The inward-facing pews of the chapel, which force the boys to see only each other during chapel services, are fitting symbols of this kind of life. Prohibited from venturing out of their house at night or from going into town, the boys are so trapped in the Byzantine rules and codes of house hierarchy (which labels juniors as "scum" and senior leaders as "whips") that their energy has to be diverted systematically into behavior that will not threaten the institution. Characteristically, such approved behavior is mostly verbal: house cheers and thumps, college slang, house names, and even a "yell of hate." The whips and class leaders seem to expend most of their energy shouting commands to "shut up" whenever the boys engage in desultory conversation. Such structured word play is, of course, one aspect of the school's system of enforced imitation (as one whip says, "If we can't set an example, who can?"). But more importantly, it is not just the school's problem but Mick's as well. His engrained response to repression during the first half of the movie is *verbal*, an unsuccessful tactic, since he is fighting the system with its own weapons; words, in *If . . .* , change nothing. Mick's innate cleverness is initially channeled into verbal defensiveness; it works in class (where he alone has no trouble answering teachers' questions), but outside the classroom he is merely a "smart mouth." There are some interesting hints in the first half of the film that Mick's words are useless: his "holiday essay" is the only one lost by Professor Stewart and even his string of baby teeth is confiscated by Denson. When he finally stops mouthing off and begins to *act*, his situation changes. His last "word" in the film is a scream (when he bayonets the chaplain), an act foreshadowed near the beginning when we first see Mick's collection of pictures: a small copy of Edvard Munch's *The Scream* is stuck on his mirror.

The boys have two alternatives to this "aping": to become like Peanuts or Mick. Peanuts hardly offers a fruitful course; he simply withdraws into the solipsistic study of invisible life (both extraterrestrial and microscopic). Mick takes the only responsible path toward liberation from the oppressive "house family"; certainly his struggle is on one level an adolescent breaking away from the protection of family to enter an unpredictable, even dangerous, world, but it is a necessary step to maturity (and one which Frank Machin never makes). "We are your new family. . . . Help the House and you'll be helped by the House," Mr. Kemp, the housemaster, tells the new arrivals, a sentiment Mick heartily rejects.

This "new family" is above all incestuous, a rarefied tribe degenerating from the lack of "new blood" in its veins. The boys see only each other; in fact, we are never acquainted with anyone from another house on campus. The references to homosexuality throughout the film, of course, work in conjunction with the emphasis on "the house"; keeping sexuality "in the family" is exactly what Mick rejects when he escapes to the Packhorse Cafe later on. The narcissism discussed earlier is a reflection of this love of self (or love of sameness), but Mick and his friends transform such narcissism into a sincere quest for individuality.

Mick enters the film in a most unusual way—he *sneaks* into it, disguised in a black overcoat, black hat, and black scarf wrapped around his mouth—a possible takeoff on Ivor Novello's character in Hitchcock's *The Lodger*, "the innocent young man," Anderson wrote, who "behaves like a stage villain."[13] Of course, he gains attention from this, which is no doubt what he wants (his need to cover up his mustache hardly warrants such an elaborate costume). He attracts attention just from the way he *looks*, he says nothing, just displays himself and observes others, provoking a variety of greetings ("Hello, Michael," "Hello, Mick," even "It's Guy Fawkes back again"). All of the boys are obsessed with names, name-calling, and self-images, and whereas the house rules require specific labels for each resident ("scum," "whip," even down to Rowntree's dictum to Jute that "You don't call me Sir"), Mick and his friends are more imaginative, devising visual names ("Bog-face," "Spotty," "Wooly-Bum") rather than the derogatory abstractions so favored by Stephans, Mick's dorm leader, and his superiors ("degenerate," "freak," "town tarts," "bloody oiks"). The whips and class leaders seem particularly annoyed with any show of self-awareness. Stephans upbraids Johnny for looking in a mirror ("Stop preening yourself in

that mirror. Preen, preen, preen, and pride"), scolds Mick for dress-
ing differently ("You're in the house now. Take that crap off") and
singing and gargling ("Stop showing off"); Denson, a whip, is obsessed with flirting ("Phillips, stop tarting") and hair lengths, telling
Mick repeatedly to get a haircut. The first thing Mick does upon
freeing himself from Stephans's attempt to unwind his muffler is
escape to his study and examine his face and newly grown mustache
in the mirror. "My face is a never-failing source of wonder to me," he
tells Johnny (who climbs over the partition and exclaims, "God,
you're ugly. You look evil"). The only boys, it turns out, who ever
look into mirrors are Mick, Johnny, and Wallace. The pin-up pictures
in the boys' studies further reveal a fascination with self-images, for
they seem to choose photos which mirror their personalities. In
contrast to the whips and Stephans, who hang pictures of the Queen,
Julie Andrews, military regiments, and castles on their walls, Mick
and his friends have almost opulent imaginations—they paper their
walls with all kinds of sexual, primitive, and revolutionary images
(nude women, guerrilla soldiers, lions, panthers; there are even two
photos of an ape in the pose of Rodin's "The Thinker," perhaps a droll
reminder of the whole evolution going on here).

Although Mick and Johnny share the same taste in pictures (both
love violent or sexual images), it is Mick who makes the final deci-
sions about which are to be taped to the walls. Johnny repeatedly asks
Mick's opinion about various pictures, as if he is not really sure of
their value. Johnny is, in fact, by far the most intellectual of the three
friends (he even wears glasses in class and professes to believe that
girls "don't think"). We first see him reading a magazine; he is rarely
without one. He spent his summer alone in the woods, "penetrating
the inner core of my being." In contrast, Mick spent his summer with
a girl, dancing and drinking in pubs, and does not ever seem to read.
He writes down his thoughts at times, yet spends most of his time
initiating activity and cutting out pictures.

Unlike Wallace and Mick, Johnny is never seen alone; it is almost
as if he cannot exist without Mick's guiding physical presence. Wallace, however, is often alone, rarely talks, and is nearly always
involved in some form of physical activity (swinging on the horizontal
bar in the gym, going to the bathroom, refereeing a rugby game). He
is never seen in class, nor do we ever see his study (we see Mick's and
Johnny's). A scene from chapter 2, set in Johnny's study, juxtaposes
the dominant qualities of each boy's personality: Johnny reads aloud
from several magazines; Wallace frets about his "rotting, senile"

body in front of a mirror, then licks a picture of a woman; Mick writes, philosophizes abstractly, then abandons it all to kiss the same picture. Burgeoning ideas, accumulating urges—the tiny room is a powderkeg of desires.

Alienation and Style

The beginning of the film, however, in no way indicates the imminent explosion—it is a calm, glassy surface, the frozen image of academia. In keeping with the world he is examining, Anderson introduces his film with an abundance of words: a song ("Stand Up!" Stand Up! For College" not only echoes one of Anderson's most controversial critical articles—"Stand Up! Stand Up!"—but shows just how far these people have "evolved" from those of Machin's world—into "upright" citizens, no less), a Bible quotation, "chapter" headings, and, of course, the credits—all against the background of a long shot freeze frame of the college. Of these, the quotation (from Proverbs 4:7) is the most ironic (as it is in *The White Bus*, where it is inscribed in the town library):

> Wisdom is the principal thing:
> therefore get wisdom:
> and with all thy getting
> get understanding.

But the "wisdom" Mick gains (in both *If . . .* and *O Lucky Man!*) is experiential, not abstract; the "wisdom" the college preaches leads only to conformity and dullness; the boys are encouraged to "understand" nothing, just obey.

In contrast, the thrust of the movie *is* toward understanding, but understanding in the Brechtian sense. And here is where so many critical problems have originated: in the mistaken notion that Anderson was tinkering with a kind of pop surrealism, using chapter titles, color shifts, and "absurd" or illogical events simply to "modernize" his story. But these techniques are just as much a part of the film as its dialogue or setting; they, in fact, make the final scene possible, so that to talk of *If . . .* as an "updating" of *Zéro de Conduite* (as many have done) is wrongheaded on several counts (if anything, the school scenes in Fellini's 1974 *Amarcord* are closer to the spirit of *If . . .*). Vigo's 1933 film did have an admitted influence on Anderson ("the debt is obvious"),[14] but his intention was not to remake the film for a sixties audience (as he once said, "I love talking about old movies and seeing old movies, but . . . if we can still see *Bringing Up Baby*, why should we bother to remake it? I call that being rather unhealthily in love with one's youth").[15] Both *If . . .* and *Zéro de Conduite* take place in repressive boys' schools, both films use chapter titles, both films focus on the rebellion of a small group of boys, and both films end with the "victorious" rebels standing atop the school buildings. But these similarities are deceptive; they obscure the important visual differences between the two movies. The black and white world of *Zéro*, in which teachers cast haunting shadows over the faces of the small boys and take on fantastic shapes and appearances, is nothing like the more mature world of *If . . .* , where not only the boys are older, but the medium is, too, so that color—whether intentionally or not—becomes an issue, and a resolution. Intellectualism and sexuality are the overwhelming passions of Anderson's teenagers, but Vigo's preadolescents are hardly so obsessed. One need only contrast the final shots of each film to appreciate fully the difference. In *Zéro* the boys stand atop a building, backs to the camera, and wave gaily down to their peers—all to the accompaniment of a happy song. In *If . . .* , the camera closes in on Mick, isolated from his friends, machine gun hammering away, his expression at once frightened, violent, and obsessed. Vigo's children face their world happily aligned; they have not destroyed it, only shaken it up by asserting their energy. Mick, however, faces a world he has destroyed; he is cut off, hardly happy, and absolutely alone. Certainly Anderson is dealing with a far different kind of rebellion; the price of intellectualism (or control) is not Vigo's major concern.

More than being just means of inducing spectator objectivity (in Brechtian terms), Anderson's techniques actually help create the final "explosion" at film's end. The chapter titles which divide the film into eight sections of declining and, finally, accelerating energy are actually rather intrusive structural devices which, like the whips' dominance in the film, seem to chop off or realign activity according to a preordained pattern. Their uselessness is obvious, for the bookishness of this world explodes right "off the page" (and what Mick and his friends do, to extend the metaphor, is "throw away the book"). Color is usually used for the opposite effect. Whenever a breaking out occurs (when doors are opened, for example), color appears, too. In this respect, the last chapter is truly liberated, for it does not revert to black and white at any point. Mick's final, explosive breakout is paralleled and intensified by the *permanence* of color—

the breakout of *our* vision from its previous limits (in contrast to the dying away of color in *The White Bus*). Of course, Anderson has said that the decision to alternate color and two-tone scenes stemmed partly from a purely economic situation: "To shoot the picture entirely in color would have meant another week on the schedule or more money on electrics."[16] But he has acknowledged, in his introduction to the screenplay of *If . . .*, that this seemingly patternless alternation of colors plays an important part in the aesthetic experience of the film:

The problem of the script seemed to be to arrive at a poetic conclusion, from a naturalistic start. (Like any fairy-story or folk-tale). We felt that variation in the visual surface of the film would help create the necessary atmosphere of poetic license. . . . I also think that, in a film dedicated to "understanding," the jog to consciousness provided by such colour change may well work a kind of healthy *Verfremdungseffect*, an incitement to *thought*, which was part of our aim. . . . There is no symbolism. . . . Only such factors as intuition, pattern, and convenience.[17]

And with true artistic ambiguity, he has allowed that the color issue may work in harmony with the liberation/repression theme ("as a result of a poetically correct instinct").[18] Certainly Anderson was not just "throwing away" the color. Early on, as a critic, he was concerned about the integration of color and style. In 1954 he remarked about some of the films showing at Cannes, "That color used to express and enrich is a desirable innovation, is obvious. At the moment, though, it tends to be too often used for its own sake."[19]

With the color–black and white alternation Anderson found a way to objectify, or "epicize," the events of the film, to make the viewers constantly aware "that they were watching a film: as indicated in the quotation at the start of *If . . .*, I was anxious that they should be on the alert, using their heads, rather than sinking back into a warm bath of emotion."[20] What all this heightened self-consciousness amounts to is that Mick, like the ideal spectator of a Brechtian epic, must confront a situation and act on his understanding of it; in other words, he must be alienated from what is going on to observe it truly. Identification with the situation will not do—hence, his initial interest in self-images becomes all the more crucial, for it is a way of distancing himself even farther from the bourgeois identity the school imposes. In Brechtian terms, Mick's *exterior* is important, not his interior; human relations, not human nature, are the issue here. (From the Brechtian vantage point, Anderson's statement that "Mick was not conceived very psychologically: he acts instinctively"[21] is more comprehensible.) Although the boys are narcissistic at first, their ultimate extroversion, or absorption in things outside the self, finally propels them right off the edge of the school's flat cosmos.

Patterns of Depletion

What begins as a potentially explosive situation ends in a temporary victory for authority in the first chapter ("Return"). Our first image of the interior of College House is alive with chaotic energy as newly arrived students scramble along a crowded corridor, colliding, arguing, and yelling (even the first words are hostile: "Machin, you bloody shag!"). By the end of the chapter the house is a tomb, a black and white (although tinted) freeze frame of a dorm room, peopled only by enlivened whispers (the tombstone-looking plaques which line the hall, then, turn out to be prophetic).

The claustrophobia of this first scene continues to compress much of the activity of the film, as the boys are packed into a myriad of cramped rooms. Moreover, the cubicles which at first glance seem private (like the bathroom stalls, the desks in the sweat room, the shower stalls, the beds in the senior dorm, and even Mick's study, which has a curtained-off area separating it from another study) are simply partitioned areas with no doors—allowing the boys to be seen by "authorities" but never to see beyond their own cubicles.

The first two scenes focus on the newcomer, Jute, the smallest and certainly most innocent boy in the house. Through him we are introduced to the house hierarchy. Jute is alone and bewildered at first, unable to see his name on a "duty list," pushed aside by everyone, jeered at, forbidden, as a "scum," to talk to older boys. His only option is to follow a herd of running boys; but he is finally assigned a "bumph tutor" and led off to the lowly sweat room, where he is introduced to a new set of regulations and "scumming lists." Almost without our realizing it, Jute becomes absorbed into the mass of undifferentiated boys and fades away as a center of interest in the film; by the end he is simply another standard bearer. He is really the first casualty in the film, a prop for the clichés and outmoded rituals of the Establishment.

While Jute and the other younger boys scamper about in confusion, Rowntree descends imperiously from his prospect atop the stairs to shout commands. With his disdainful, intellectual bearing, Rowntree is a direct descendant of Mr. Weaver in *This Sporting Life* and a forebear of Sir James in *O Lucky Man!*, a strange breed of creatures who slide through life with supercilious ease. These characters rarely engage in physical activity, preferring instead to deliver opinions and orders from some pinnacle of authority. Rowntree is so detached, in fact, that he commands his scum to "warm a lavatory seat for me. I'll be ready in three minutes." He owns plenty of "elitist" sporting equipment (golf clubs and tennis rackets which he packs in an Ancient Age box), but we never see him use it. As if this were not enough, we even hear that Rowntree spent his summer in India: it was "jolly good."

"When do we live, that's what I want to know," Mick asks Johnny in chapter 1, and the first half of the film echoes the question in its very structure. From Rowntree's commands, to Machin's supervision in the sweat room, to Stephans's petty orders in the dorm, to, finally, the Matron's inspection and the whips' bedtime check, every stray impulse is brought under control—and, appropriately, every chapter ends in either fatigue or repression. Spontaneity has been scrubbed from the agenda of the school by an incredible countdown system: "Dormitory inspection in three minutes!" "You've got thirty minutes to get out," "Junior exercise lists up in five minutes!" Every activity has a preordained time and place based on "centuries of tradition." As Mr. Kemp says in his welcome-back address, "Work—play—but don't mix the two," an explicit enough description of the imperialistic compulsion to divide and fragment experience. It is that old familiar division of labor that we saw in *This Sporting Life*, only instead of a society which assigns unchanging roles to people (workers and thinkers), we find here a society of people who are divided *within* themselves, encouraged to develop, but never to integrate, their physical and mental abilities. Stephans is a product of this way of thinking, ordering Peanuts to take his telescope out of the dorm (mistaking it for "a bloody ray gun"); similarly, Whip Barnes orders Jute to remove his diary from the dorm, for no other reason than that it does not *belong* there. Items and activities are categorized to the point of absurdity—there is no room here for the overlap or convergence of *anything* important.

In such a divisive environment, hostility is never absent—it is the emotional bedrock of the system; without it the structure of the place would collapse (and the irony, of course, is that the hostility which is built into the system guarantees its fall). The verbal warfare of the first scene continues, with Jute's tutor telling him, "You've got to know all the Seniors' names," only to be silenced and cursed by a whip. A line of boys passes a message down to the last boy: "Biles, why are you a freak?" Rowntree warns that he will "come crashing down" on anyone manifesting a "deplorable lack of spirit" and details the "lock-up" schedule of the house. The boys are interrogated about "eye disease" and "V.D." (rather interesting—albeit ridiculous— areas of concern for an institution of blindness and sexual repression) and must undergo a flashlight genital inspection by the matron (the first overt manifestation of the kinkiness of an inbred system).

As the boys get ready for bed, the first black and white scene (in sepia tint) appears as Mrs. Kemp shows the new teacher, Mr. Thomas, to his tiny, cramped attic room, which can only be reached, ludicrously, by a long climb up a narrow staircase. The lack of color, coupled with the sight of poor Mr. Thomas slumped over on his bed as Mrs. Kemp leaves him in this apparently unheated cell to contemplate "the church spire," creates one of the most visually imprisoning scenes in the movie, as Anderson shows just how much *worse* the adults have it than the children. They are raised to accept confinement, and they do so. As Paul Pennyfeather realizes in *Decline and Fall*, "Anyone who has been to an English public school will always feel comparatively at home in prison. It is the people brought up in the gay intimacy of the slums . . . who find prison so soul destroying."[22]

Color returns when the scene cuts back to the dorms, but as the chapter ends light, color, motion, and even people disappear. The house lights go off, a tinted freeze frame of the darkened senior dorm appears, and we hear the boys whisper about sex and religion until Peanuts closes the subject by saying, "Paradise is for the blessed— not for the sex-obsessed."

The repressed energy of chapter 1 finds sadistic outlets in chapter 2, as the boys and their masters engage in various forms of torture. The chapter begins with the college assembled in chapel, each house in a separate section (all houses facing inward), the women isolated in a balcony. The segregation of women throughout the film is another subtle reminder of just how artificial this "civilized" world is. There almost seems to be a kind of purdah in effect, for girls are not even permitted to join in any of the boys' extracurricular activities. As one boy says, girls have been banned from the orchestra for being "temptations of the devil." Mrs. Kemp's lonely walk through the deserted dorm later on deepens this chasm between the sexes; while the men are involved in war games, the sole "youngish" woman in the school wanders naked in the halls.

The headmaster, as we see in this chapter, is a master of double-talk, glibly orating about values and education and saying, essentially, nothing. While he and Mr. Stewart talk a great deal about "imagination" and "creativeness," there is no evidence of these qualities here. The whips trail behind the headmaster like obsequious lackeys, visually denying the headmaster's claim that "there are boys in college in whom the muscles of creativeness are flexing, the pinions of imagination twitching." When confronted with boys who *are* flexing creative muscles (namely, Mick, Johnny, and Wallace), he assigns them a good dose of the Protestant work ethic to rid their systems of rebellion. As the headmaster rhapsodizes about the need for "middle class values," the camera rests on an idle groundsman; the men sweep by without even noticing him. Old statues, frozen into niches of a building, and uniformed, marching cadets provide the background for the headmaster's pompous exclamation that "Britain today is a powerhouse . . . of ideas, experiments, imagination." But inflexible, unable to respond to challenges, the school—or any bureaucratic or highly structured system—can only pretend to change by giving lip service to fashion (as the headmaster does throughout the film, saying such things as, "Of one thing I'm certain: short hair is no indication of merit"). Because of its inability to move into the twentieth century, the college stays mired in antiquity, as Anderson suggests by cutting to a painting of a college founder (sporting a "shrewd, Tudor look")[23] after the headmaster claims that college is "an exciting place."

The only excitement in this chapter results from the bursts of pent-up adolescent energy. When the younger boys are released from chapel, they literally run up the walls of a corridor and, later, torture the unfortunate Biles by hanging him upside down above a toilet and plunging his head into the flushing water. The latter is a fitting introduction to the final scene of the chapter, in which Stephans confesses his "dirty thoughts" to the chaplain. The chaplain's exhortation to "fight the good fight," followed by a shot of his "fatherly" hand upon Stephans's bowed head, closes a particularly "head-centered" chapter. Earlier in the chapter the chaplain hits a boy's head in math class and twists Jute's nipple to elicit a correct answer; the battered boy, in turn, puts Jute through an angry catechism of house slang (which must be "word perfect" to avoid getting a beating). Biles's "head-washing" in the toilet is, then, the final comment on the degenerate ways the system "brainwashes" its initiates.

In contrast to these scenes, we find Mick, alone in his study, playing his primitive "Sanctus" record over and over and cutting out pictures of wild animals for his wall collage. While he is infatuated with primal energy, he is nevertheless inactive, simply *finding* images instead of *creating* them, and listening to repeated sounds on his record (in this respect, imitating the others in their endless college and chapel songs, although after his motorcycle adventure he never again plays the record).

The third chapter ("Term Time"), like the two before it, begins with a burst of activity that grinds to a halt. The rugby players collapse in a huddle, and by the end of the chapter all we see is Mick standing under a cold shower, shivering and defeated. The whips dominate this chapter with their increasingly forceful display of prissy power. Their authority is being undermined, however, by their own pettiness and cruelty, while the other boys grow more united. The swallowing-up of little Jute may be a victory for the system, but Bobby Phillips's "radicalization" is a far more significant reversal. The most physically exploited boy in the house (who is feminized by the whips into a caricature of a "blond tart"), Phillips does not openly object when Rowntree "gives" him to Denson as a sexual temptation. But he "abandons" Denson to rendezvous with the traitorous Wallace (in an armory, no less—potential energy is everywhere) and finally joins the rebels at film's end, helping to blast away at parents, masters, and whips, and, most importantly, rejecting his status as the object of a clammy, repressed lust.

The whips' attempts to extend their control are contrasted in the first part of the chapter with the uncontrolled impulses of their "subjects." As the film cuts back and forth from Phillips's lively, merry group to the priggish whips, it becomes hard to believe that the whips are only children themselves—just a few years older than the juniors. And when we cut from their barren, "civilized" room to Johnny's study, the contrast is astounding. Surrounded by bright colors and photographs of women, Mick and his friends seem not only *young*, but far more interested in ideas and events outside the confines of the school ("In Calcutta somebody dies of starvation every eight minutes") than in the petty squabbles of the whips (even though, to be sure, their interest smacks of a rather detached fascination). Denson invades Mick's "territory" to dole out cold shower punishments for "long hair" and alcohol possession and confiscates Mick's string of teeth. The confiscation, as previously pointed out, raises an interesting problem with Mick, for his rebellion throughout

the first half of the movie takes the form of futile verbal volleys hurled
at the whips and strikingly haughty behavior, indications that he can
only *react* to his environment, employing the same weapons it uses
against him (for Rowntree and Denson use words and haughtiness
with equal temerity). As Johnny tells him in this scene, "No matter
how strong the urge, resist any temptation to go into battle this
month. Otherwise you run the risk of not only being on the wrong
side, but possibly the wrong war." The whips single out Mick for
extra punishment because he is the most verbal of the rebels, the one
who initially fights only with hostile words. Thus his extra time under
the cold shower at the end of the chapter stems, at least partially,
from his having to have the last word: "My time's up, you bastard."
The chapter ends, like those before it, in an image of physical
repression: Mick's hunched, shivering back under the shower.

Patterns of Freedom

This pattern is broken in the next chapter, however. It begins—
instead of ends—with regulated inactivity (as the college is assembled in chapel to hear Rowntree's sermon) and works through to
physical freedom (the motorcycle excursion); in fact, all of the re-
maining chapters will follow this pattern of energy accretion. As the
title, "Ritual and Romance," suggests, the chapter is a turning point
in the film, for here we find a series of almost archetypal rites of
passage for the boys: a "make-believe" medieval duel (in which "real
blood" is drawn), a Western-style adventure in the Packhorse Cafe,
street fighting (with invisible razors), and an awakening sexuality (for
Phillips and Wallace as well as for Mick and the café girl). While the
war games the boys play are, on the one hand, extensions of the
hostility found on every level of the school (and which, psychologically, provide a release for the pent-up frustrations of the boys), their
historical nature (especially evident in the duel, as they yell such
phrases as "England awake!" "We are not cotton-spinners all!" and
"Death to tyrants!") might imply that the boys are not only fantasizing
their actions, but idealizing them as well, performing their skits
against a backdrop of castles and saloons and looking to the myths of
those times to find formulas for behavior. Before they escape to town,
their fantasy is nationalistic ("Some love England and her honour
yet!"); when they steal a motorcycle and ride to the café, however,
they become swaggering outlaws, representing nothing but them-

Archetypal rites of passage for the rebels in If . . . ; (top) Malcolm McDowell, David Wood and Richard Warwick duelling; (bottom) with the girl at the Packhorse Cafe.

selves. Finally, they have their own grievances to avenge, rather than mythological ones, and must act spontaneously. Of course, the boys are dressed as modern guerrilla fighters at the end of the movie, but they have at least moved imaginatively into the twentieth century, while the system they are shooting at is still locked in antiquity.

The first breakout of the chapter occurs when Mick and Johnny escape to town in handcuffs like fugitives from a chain gang (and in violation of Rowntree's order to attend the rugby match and "cheer—loudly"). But there are other breakouts. Three bursts of color (from tinted black and white) appear when doors are opened (after chapel; during the duel; and when Mick, Johnny, and the girl go outside the café to ride on the motorcycle)—each time correlating visual freedom with physical freedom. Wallace's graceful acrobatics on the horizontal bar are a break with the structured, awkward vault-jumping of the juniors (as well as with the school's tacit policy of bodily abhorrence). In addition, Mick, Johnny, and Wallace literally break out of the film frames; Mick and Johnny run out of our field of vision when they first enter the town, and Wallace flies through the air after his gymnastic exercise, leaving the camera focused on an empty gym.

The escape into town offers more than physical freedom; it shows Mick's awakening to images outside his carefully arranged collage—first to the shop windows full of "forbidden" items (women's underclothes and cars), then to the expanding horizon of the countryside as he and Johnny take a long ride on the stolen motorcycle, and finally to the café girl, who challenges Mick to "look at me" and talks about her eyes "growing bigger and bigger" in the mirror. Mick not only looks at her (and, in his own narcissistic style, "preens" in a mirror when he enters the café), but wrestles animal-style (and eventually naked) with her on the floor, all to the accompaniment of his "Sanctus." Everything about this sequence violates college values. Even the comic Western elements here (the name of the café; Mick's treatment of his motorcycle as if it were a favored horse; the slot machines in the café; and the stylized, almost caricatured behavior of Mick and the girl, as they parody the "stranger in town meeting hardened saloon girl" scenario) serve to remove the adventure from the stranglehold of the rarified Establishment—into, possibly, the world of drama and imagination. But the real slap to the Old World is inherent in the motion and freedom of the cycle ride, the theft of private property, the association with the girl (whom the others would describe as a "town tart"), and, of course, the sexual energy. The latter, Anderson has noted, "has something of the same impact of the revolution at the end" since it "suggests the link between sex and freedom, the relationship between sex and anarchy, if you like—the emotional and liberating quality that there is, or should be, in sex."[24]

While Mick's experiences have been divided into the "real" and the "ideal" (discussing, for example, what to do with fantasy women), this scene marks the dissolution of such fragmentation, seeming at once realistic and fantastic. Many critics have expressed bewilderment (and even hostility) over this scene, wondering continually, "Does the café scene 'really' happen?" But this reaction is precisely at odds with all Mick—and the film—tries to accomplish. Of course it happens; it is, as Anderson has said, "all real":[25] "I wouldn't like to say, 'Now it's *fantasy*. Now it's *real*.' Because the whole point of fantasy is that it *is* real. And that there aren't in life any rigid distinctions between what is real and what is fantasy. Our fantasies are *part* of our reality."[26] And in this vein, Anderson has quoted Brecht to bolster his claim that *If* . . . is a realistic film: "Realism is not a matter of showing real things, but of showing how things really are."[27] The categories of experience so dear to the college administrators are just what this scene aims to dissolve. From this point on in the movie, "fantasy" becomes more and more intertwined with "reality," and Mick can only move farther from the confines of the college, for he no longer shares its mentality, no longer segregates experience into "work" and "play" schedules. His experience with the girl sets him even farther apart from the others, for he is the one person in the film who makes real contact with women, in itself a dramatic breaking out.

Appropriately, the next chapter begins with a shot of the sweat room from *outside* a window, as the camera, like Mick, now becomes progressively distanced from the college. Rowntree's monitoring of the sweat room and Denson's bivouac outside seem all the more ridiculous in light of Mick's adventure, yet when we next see him he is testing his endurance by trying to breathe with a plastic bag wrapped around his head. Back in the old claustrophobic routine, the boys are preoccupied with death. The "worst ways to die" that they discuss (being flayed and suffering an eaten-up brain) exist around them in the very structure of the school, both metaphorically (in the school's insistence on outmoded, meaningless rituals and verbal codes which destroy individual intelligence) and literally (in the beatings—or "flayings"—the boys receive at the end of the chapter). Their obsession is justified, not paranoid: death *is* the situation.

Anderson has said that Mick, Johnny, and Wallace "are beaten for what they are . . . rather than to tie everything together in a specific cause and effect."[28] Rowntree (whose avowed intention is to quell the "unruly elements" who "threaten the stability of the House") tells the boys they are to be beaten for their "general attitude," and Denson singles out Mick for his appearance, which somehow threatens the militaristic conformity of the house: "There's something indecent about you, Travis. The way you slouch about . . . with your hands in your pockets. The way you just *sit* there looking at everyone. . . . You can take that cheap little grin off your mouth! (grasping the emblem on his blazer) 'I serve the nation!' '" Mick, still fighting the system with its own weapons, strikes back verbally ("You mean that piece of wool on your tit?") and ensures a more severe beating for himself.

The beatings signal a second turning point in Mick's behavior, showing him, as Anderson has suggested, not only what he *is* (as far as the school is concerned) but the futility of simply flinging words about. "Mouthing off" changes nothing, for, as the leaders of the school have shown all along, they are more adept at it than Mick. As if to underscore Mick's development, Anderson, during the beating scene, searches out Peanuts, the retiring boy who so far has attracted attention only for possessing a telescope. In his study cubicle, surrounded by pictures of babies in wombs, planets, and stars, Peanuts examines a slide through his microscope. While hearing the crack of Rowntree's whip on Mick's backside, we see the magnified cells divide and multiply rapidly under the microscope. This scene (the final one in the chapter), reflects not only the *inner* growth that Mick experiences as a result of the beating, but one of the major problems of the mentality of the school—its detachment, its refusal to deal with reality. Peanuts is fascinated by the unborn, the distant, the nearly invisible—in short, he is the perfect student. This scene, further, parallels the final scene of the next chapter in which Peanuts offers Mick a look at the heavens through his telescope.

While the whips earnestly translate a passage from Plato's *Republic*, Mick shoots darts at the pictures he has painstakingly displayed. Not only are the whips faced by a bust of Demosthenes (a paragon of verbal power), but they are involved in translating Platonic ideas. Words, antiquity, and idealism all contrast here with Mick's new activist (and *silent*) behavior, as he strikes out at a way of life he has outgrown. The enclosed world of his study, carefully lined with selected images, can no longer contain a person acutely aware of the world outside its walls. As Peanuts tells Mick at the end of the chapter, "Space, you see, Michael, is all-expanding at the speed of light."

Another juxtaposition occurs after the dining room scene in which Rowntree directs the boys to give the "House Thump" (and from which Mick, Johnny, and Wallace are noticeably absent), when the rebels pledge their commitment to "the Resistance" and "Liberty!" with a blood pact. Mick now claims that "one man can change the world—with a bullet in the right place" (and this comment is followed by a shot of his photograph of Lenin in peasant disguise which looks amazingly like Mick), and his obvious authority over the other boys (telling them to "trust me" and to attack "when I say") shows that while he is the most active and responsible member of the group, he nevertheless is still fighting the system with its own weapons (i.e., organizing militaristically to destroy a militaristic structure), perhaps engaging in his own dream of power. On another level, however, Mick's behavior is representative of the "seeds of destruction" sown by an inherently destructive system, for like the bombs created at the atomic plant in *O Lucky Man!* which explode prematurely, the hostile young soldiers spawned by the school eventually turn on their masters.

Despite the vestiges of intellectualism Mick still possesses, he has evolved far beyond the abstractionist mentality of those around him. His "real bullets" come from outside his window (he has kept them on the ledge), although we never learn where he originally got them. What is important is simply the fact that Mick is reaching *out* of his room and that the "outside world" furnishes him with the tools to defeat his oppressors. Windows, in fact, are important indicators of breaking out and looking beyond in the film; this is particularly noticeable in the camera's move to the *outsides* of buildings at the beginnings of the later chapters (as opposed to the interior shots of windows which characterize the beginnings of the first three chapters), as it, along with Mick, becomes distanced from the college. Mick is the only one of the boys who leans out of the dorm window to look around and breathe in the night air, and it is he who, at the end of the chapter, brings Peanuts's telescope lens down from its focal point in the stars (where the boy is sure another English-speaking planet exists) toward the more inscrutable Earth, focusing on the café girl as she sits in a window brushing her hair. Her acknowledgment of the telescope, besides being another of Anderson's purposely "ambiguous" scenes which dissolve reality and fantasy into "imaginative freedom,"[29] establishes eye contact with Mick and suggests, as they both peer out the windows at each other, Mick's association with everything the school denies. Furthermore, the girl's mysterious acknowledgment foreshadows Michael's awareness of the camera at the end of *O Lucky Man!*; she is, in essence, conscious of her own image. While the boys in school have been grappling with self-images, defining themselves according to house hierarchy and pinning each other with derogatory labels, the girl is the character most at ease with simply being what she is, a stage Michael/Mick will not reach until the end of *O Lucky Man!*

The war games in the next chapter become, within this context, not just outlets for repressed energy or reflections of the violence inherent in an imperialistic system, but expressions of the warped self-images fostered by the school. Divided into armies, the cadets and masters play at murder and terror, inspired by the chaplain to see themselves as crusaders for Christ. Although the boys are taught the importance of the "yell of hate," the sound, like all of the other required sounds in the school, is simply artifice. This is especially clear when Mick gives his own yell of hate (his last "word" in the film) as he bayonets the chaplain. As the person who, more than any other, represents the values of the school, the chaplain is an appropriate initial "casualty" in the war against oppression. Whether or not Mick "actually" kills the chaplain seems beside the point, for his actions and "yell of hate" terrorize a community unused to authenticity and for whom such acts are merely anemic contrivance. Furthermore, when the headmaster rolls the chaplain out of a cabinet later on, it is only to hear the boys' apologies, a clear satirization of the role of religion in the institution: to hear and "sanctify" words. But Mick no longer plays at war (as he did in his duels and street fights); he refuses to dwell in a world of idealized or fake action. The headmaster, however, fashionable liberal that he is, ignores the physical reality of what has happened on the "battlefield" and tries to place Mick's actions in a framework of trendy ideas: "It's a natural characteristic of adolescence to want to proclaim individuality . . . . It's a quite blameless form of existentialism. This, for instance, is what lies at the heart of the great hair problem. . . . Now, you boys are . . . too intelligent to be rebels. That's too easy. And it would be easy to punish you in the normal way. But I'm going to give you a privilege: work. Real work."

If Mick were still behaving as he did in the first half of the movie (by, perhaps, talking back to the headmaster), his "punishment" would seem severe. But stripped of his indolent intellectual pose, he now thrives on action, and the headmaster's command to clean out the attics and storerooms of the college leads to Mick's discovery of the ammunition that destroys both the headmaster and his institution.

Anderson has described the boys' "house-cleaning" as an eradication of "the dust of centuries of traditions that have just gone moldy and been forgotten or neglected, however much lip service has been paid to them."[30] Appropriately, the items the boys burn in a bonfire are symbolic of the school (and are found, ironically, in the very hall which holds the Founders Day celebrants in the next chapter): stuffed animals, an upside-down map of the British Empire, moldy flags and books. The fetus the boys find is, of course, even more representative of the fate of children whose growth is stunted by repressive institutions and mentalities (most notably, Jute). What is most important here, though, is the sequence of events, for although the boys are confronted with a possible self-image (the most chilling one in the film), the café girl appears inexplicably and locks it away in its rotting cupboard. After this they discover a cache of ammunition, and there seems to be no question at this point how it will be used. Just as Mick discovers his own potential for action, so does he discover the vaulted energy of the school (unleashing it in the final scene).

Anarchy: The Triumph of Action

The last chapter begins with a zoom-out from the Union Jack atop the College Hall, the first shot of its kind in the movie and one which shows the camera's continuing movement away from the college and its symbols. A zoom-in to Mick's face occurs later, allying him with the camera, individuating him, and presaging the iris-in to Michael at the end of *O Lucky Man!* The violence which finally erupts in this sequence occurs on Founders Day, as the benefactors, masters, parents, and symbolically dressed characters (three knights in armor, a bishop, an army general, and some sort of royal-looking woman—all that "gold filling in a mouthful of decay," to use John Osborne's phrase) are gathered to celebrate the establishment of the school.

Before introducing the general (Denson's father, perhaps?), the headmaster rhapsodizes most ironically about the college: "There can be few places where tradition is examined with such a critical eye as this college. A constant self-appraisal is going on, and indeed, changes are happening so fast that even as I speak, these words are out of date." While he believes his pseudo-liberal rhetoric reflects progressive change, the "critical eye" of "self-appraisal" has been Mick's; the headmaster's words have been "out of date" all along, and changes are indeed happening as he speaks, for the rebels are about to set fire to the hall. As General Denson delivers a rousing oration in praise of "privilege . . . tradition . . . discipline . . . obedience" and "England, our England" which "doesn't change so easily," the stage beneath him begins to smolder. As befits one who will not recognize change, the general is the last person in the hall to see the smoke and shouts unnoticed orders to the herd of fleeing guests.

The crowd is hit with gunfire and explosions as they pour onto the courtyard. The camera zooms-in to discover Mike, the café girl, Johnny, Wallace, and Phillips on a rooftop, shooting and tossing grenades at the patrons, who mobilize rapidly into fighting positions (as if they were old hands at it!). Mick's actions have finally roused others to action and the long-suppressed energy of the place erupts into *real* warfare.

Although many people fall to the ground, only two recognizable "dignitaries" are "killed" in the course of the film: the chaplain (whose strange reappearance marks his "death" at Mick's hands as plainly metaphoric) and the headmaster. As the most stubborn obstacle to change, the headmaster must die if Mick's battle is to have any constructive meaning. His final appeal to rationality ("Listen to reason and trust me!") is, by this time, futile: the café girl shoots him between the eyes. As if he never really possessed a body, the headmaster seems to disappear in a puff of smoke, leaving behind only a scorched patch of ground.

After this, the rest of the loyalists rush forward and the movie ends in the middle of battle. Mick is still shooting, his "desperate, unyielding"[31] face (with its rather ambiguous expression of terror and obsession) the last image of the film. Anderson has said that "if you really look at the last scene of *If* . . . you can't really think that Mick is triumphant," and it would be hard indeed to interpret the final shot as unqualified glorification of Mick's rebellion. To Anderson, Mick is a "romantic hero at bay,"[32] one who has fought "the good fight" but who is probably destined to fail ("The world rallies as it always will and brings its overwhelming firepower to bear on the man who says 'No.' ").[33] As for the role of anarchy in all of this, Anderson claims that *If* . . . is "deeply anarchistic" because "people persistently misunderstand the term anarchistic, and think it just means wildly chucking bombs about, but anarchy is a social and political philosophy which puts the highest possible value on responsibility. The notion of somebody who wants to change the world is not the notion of an irresponsible person."[34]

David Sherwin's view of Mick, though, is more severe: "In order to act, in order to free himself from the evil and corruption about him, he is turned into a monster himself. . . . This is what happens to Mick. He becomes as evil and as terrible at the end as the headmaster or the general."[35] A bleak view indeed, and one which suggests that every revolution inevitably turns fascistic, every actor becomes a reactor. There is evidence for this in the film, especially in Mick's growing authoritarian behavior (and even in *O Lucky Man!* where Mick next appears as a passive tool of various imperialistic systems). Certainly in light of the Kipling poem "If " (from which Anderson got the film's title), Mick's position is ambiguous: "If you can keep your head while others around you are losing theirs . . . you'll be a man, my son." Mick *has* kept his head, but at what price? Sherwin's view does not take into account Mick's lack of control at the end, the fact that his machine gun seems almost to be shooting itself, jostling Mick about like a puppet. We cannot forget that Mick has made progress in the film, for he is no longer the dilettantish rebel who was so fascinated by "real blood" and "real bullets," talked of death and war in romantic, abstract phrases, and thought in terms of ultimate, final acts (like "The whole world will end very soon—black brittle bodies peeling into ash. . . . War is the last possible creative act," or "There's only one thing you can do with a girl like this [pointing to a picture.] . . . Walk naked into the sea together as the sun sets, make love once, then die"). At least he now *acts*. This is not an evil boy, but simply one who has taken sincere physical action and in so doing has unleashed all the violent energy of the school (and, by extension, the system it represents); he has exploded, in John Osborne's inimitable words from the fifties, "the protocol of ancient fatuity."[36] He has, in effect, energized the movie, given it form. Mick's postrevolution psychological state is not really the point; the carrying through of an impulse or instinct *is*. As Anderson says, "If his story can be said to be 'about' anything, it is about freedom."[37]

But a world beyond Mick's cause is, of course, conceivable, and as the character Michael in *O Lucky Man!* he will descend—literally—into the postwar world. In contrast to the many high-angle shots used in *If . . .* , and Mick's elevation atop the college building at film's end, the "falling camera" of *O Lucky Man!* suggests that Mick's rather detached position is ultimately untenable and that he must "fall to earth." The two Micks are quite different characters, but they are allies in a crusade for not only *personal* freedom, but *narrative* and aesthetic liberty as well, for *O Lucky Man!* carries the "revolution" begun in *If . . .* to its logical, and most explosive, culmination.

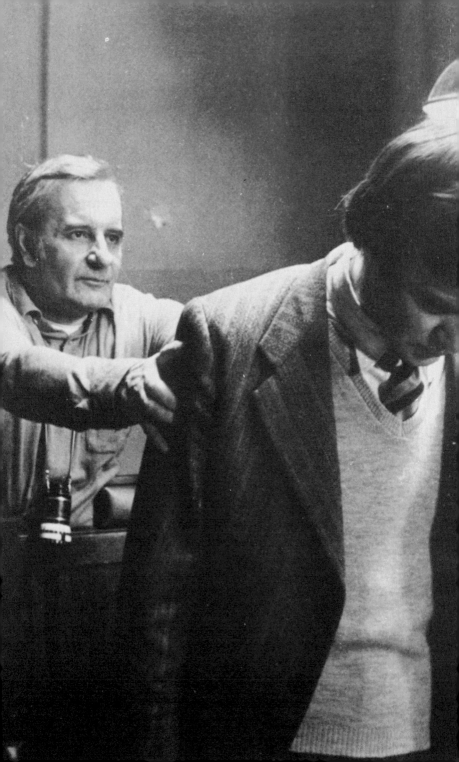

6

The Epic Structure of
O Lucky Man!:
New Identities, New Images

"PERHAPS there is a sense of impatience with the old forms," Anderson noted in reference to *O Lucky Man!* "Or if not impatience, at least a feeling that there are certain kinds of truth, certain kinds of experience, which they are no longer able to convey. I think very likely I was struggling towards the expression of some such feeling."[1] The "sense of impatience" is never more obvious than in the final scenes of the movie. Michael Travis wanders into what he thinks is an audition hall to try out for a role in a movie, yet when a clapper board reading "O LUCKY MAN!, Scene 755" snaps across his face as he poses for photographs, we are reminded that what he has walked into is, of course, simply another scene in *O Lucky Man!* The word "simply" is perhaps misleading, though, for this scene is one of the most significant in all of Anderson's work; in a way, it is a brilliant realization of his impatience with "old forms," and the final, successful blow to Michael's naive assumption that life—and art—are finished products, "dished up" for the titillation of passive onlookers. The culinary metaphor is not inappropriate here, for consumption is a major interest of the film. Anderson has said that "although my point of view is not Marxist, I shouldn't think there have been many more Brechtian films than *O Lucky Man!*"[2] but Brechtian, as he suggests, not in a narrowly political sense (for the film is certainly not Marxist), but in a broader, aesthetic sense. Anderson is obviously a conspirator in the rebellion against what Brecht called the "culinary theatre," or that "branch of the bourgeois drug traffic"[3] which simply lays out dramatic goodies for the mindless consumption of the audience. Michael's "progress through illusion"[4] (as Anderson calls it) is, in essence, a journey through the *theater* of illusion, for what is Michael if not a consumption-minded spectator in every sequence but the last two, a pleased-as-punch lackey who identifies with nearly any person or cause that promises to keep his belly full? Of all the political, social, and eventually even aesthetic misconceptions he holds, his most disastrous illusion is that life is a groaning sideboard of treats served up to those who merely open their mouths and smile.

Michael is certainly rewarded often enough: he is virtually innundated with food for most of the movie (fed coffee as if he were a baby bird; given cheese and Scotch as bribes; repeatedly offered meals, mints, apples, and drinks; and even breastfed!). But he is similarly glutted to near insensibility with ideas and commands from others. Only when he is denied physical and moral sustenance and is starving, in pain, and alienated from everything he once revered does he begin to question his actions and actually observe his world. His ultimate discovery (recognizing not only the camera which has been following him throughout the film[5] but the fact that he is, indeed, *being watched*, and is a creator—not a recipient—of life) seems to transform immediately the dreary, "unemployed" actors in the audition hall into colorful dancers and, in effect, to revolutionize the course of the film.

But the "magic story"[6] of this revelation is a particularly tricky directorial feat, since the narrative always stays at once realistic and fantastic. Brechtian techniques come into play, and like the intermittent color in *If . . .* and *The White Bus*, the titles, captions, and songs in *O Lucky Man!* are dramatic alienating devices. But it is Malcolm McDowell's portrayal of Michael which most deeply effects the distancing process. "For me," Anderson reflected shortly after the film's release, "the extraordinary quality of Malcolm McDowell's performance in this film is to ring so many changes on innocence. And to keep a character who is most of the time reacting continuously dynamic and interesting."[7] To be sure, it is amazing that such a vapid character can be so compelling and screen-worthy; McDowell's Mick, in *If . . .* , for example, is far more "accessible" to an audience. But this issue of identification instigated McDowell's own problems with the role. Throughout the filming of *O Lucky Man!* Anderson tried to elicit a "realistic style of acting, as opposed to a naturalistic style, which is more what is commonly thought of as film acting,"[8] and this rather Brechtian notion of realism ("not a matter of showing real things, but of showing how things really are")[9] is, of course, at odds with any kind of acting in which (in Anderson's words) "we can see the actors making their choices."[10] From the beginning, Michael Travis was a challenge to McDowell. David Sherwin, in his "Diary" of the script, recalls McDowell finding Michael "a sheep, too passive. . . . He needs a bit more go—don't you think?"[11] (an interesting problem in light of the fact that McDowell had the original idea for the script, based on his experiences as a coffee salesman in the north of England). Anderson (who told him, "You've got to pretend to be naive; it's how you were ten years ago")[12] found that McDowell's greatest acting challenge stemmed from the fact that "everyone else was playing—not caricatures but sharply defined characters, almost . . . 'humours.' He was playing someone that was the centre of the film, and yet with whom the audience must be able to identify, so that he could not be bizarre or caricatured at all. And yet is was obvious that he could never afford to fall back on mere behaviour. When he did, it never rang true, and we had to stop and start again. . . . It's the kind of part which has to create its own dynamic, because it doesn't come from anything else."[13]

This absence of psychological identification is particularly Brechtian in its refusal to assign fixed, immutable personalities to characters and its acceptance of identity change as an inescapable consequence of social and economic realities. Anderson once claimed that the words "parable" or "fable" were more "humane"[14] descriptions of alienating works of art. Given not only the finesse of McDowell's performance, but the wonderfully subtle recurrence of actors in different roles (who "have to present themselves completely the moment they appear"),[15] we can see that Anderson has created what he would describe as an "epic satire" which "accommodates itself to a film of ideas rather than to the more traditional kind of film which is based on a closely worked out plotline or psychological study of the characters . . . working out the whole thing in terms of ideas rather than personalities."[16]

The structure Anderson chose for his epic satire, a series of episodes and adventures which occur "along the road," is highly picaresque. Michael, of course, seems every bit the traditional picaro: a conniving, sometimes charming, opportunistic, and essentially conformist outcast. Even his name, "Travis," suggests a "traversing," or journey (he is, in fact, mistakenly called "Travers" in his first appearance). But while the satirical nature of picaresque narratives is obvious (and is certainly applicable to *O Lucky Man!*), one of the most interesting aspects of such a genre is its implicit concern with social and psychological disintegration. For all the picaro's comic escapades, the motivating force behind his progress is not a desire to denigrate his society but to *join* it. Despite his continual discovery of corruption and hypocrisy in his superiors, the picaro will usually do anything—even negate whatever uniqueness he possesses—to win their acceptance. Michael's adventures are episodes in his possible growth, but he always reneges, always "smiles," and always finds himself on a dead-end of potential and vitality.

Throughout the film, each system Michael confronts, whether it be commercial or scientific, thrives on reducing life to objects manipulatable by an aristocracy of experts; even art is vulnerable to the same control, for Anderson himself becomes the last of a line of "directors" who try to manipulate Michael in some way. But Michael's rejection of his role as a robotlike boy who is acted upon, and subsequent metamorphosis into a self-motivated actor, galvanize the film. Moviemaking alone emerges from the calamitous cycles of technological and industrial failures as a vital, life-enhancing process; in fact, everything breaks down except the movie itself, which actually *acquires* energy and erupts ultimately in celebration. Real progress only begins when Michael confronts his own nothingness, thereby affirming, in the Zen overtones of so much of *O Lucky Man!*, his infinite fullness.

As the story of the growth of this type of self-awareness, the film chronicles both Michael's birth as a star (and, by extension, his development of individuality and rebellion against bourgeois notions of success) and *O Lucky Man!*'s birth as a movie. While every movie could be said to tell the story of its own birth, what we see and hear in the first three sequences of *O Lucky Man!* is a "mini-history" of the entire course of the film. On the soundtrack of the first sequence, a silent melodrama entitled "Once Upon a Time," is only the clatter of a running movie projector; the story here is projected as a "finished product." During the second "modern" sequence ("Now"), we are even more aware of movie technology, for the roving cameras occupy almost as much space as Alan Price and his band; Anderson's presence here reinforces the "movie in progress" appearance of the sequence. Beginning with the tracking shot of the third sequence, though, which introduces Michael's story, we no longer hear or see movie apparatus; in fact, we seem to be "behind" the camera we last saw tracking out of Price's studio. Whereas we first heard a projector, then saw a scene being filmed, we are now primarily aware of the image itself. The movement in these first three sequences from projector- to camera- to lens-consciousness (or, in other words, from "product" to "process") suggests a progressive denial of passivity and vicarious experience in favor of involvement—exactly the same pattern Michael's progress will follow. Similarly, the historical perspective set up in the first two sequences—the leap from "then" to "now"—is minimized and finally destroyed, as Michael learns that the only way to escape history (or at least the control of the present by the past) is to live in the present and to be alive to everything around him. Linearity gives way to circularity, causality gives way to spontaneity, and experience becomes creative, not consumptive.

Setting the Stage

Immediately following the opening title ("Once Upon a Time"), we see an irising-out of the camera lens from one coffee plantation worker to his surrounding workers in the field, a shot which suggests the awakening Michael must experience in order to break out of what turns out to be a highly repetitive existence. The lens, however, has opened upon an oppressive, imperialistic world. Only the authority figure, a uniformed guard, stands and moves. And only the authority figure is visually alert, spying a peasant stealing coffee beans before the peasant detects his presence. The fact that Malcolm McDowell plays the roles of both Michael and the peasant links the characters in a partnership of insensitivity, for they share a blindness to their surroundings and a subservience to a system of controlling figures that seem to doom them to obscurity or failure. But while the peasant is trapped in his melodrama, Michael is not, for the rest of the movie works ultimately to liberate him from the restrictions of this initial sequence.

Entrenched in dramatic conventions and clichés, this Russian-style montage of "meaningful" gestures and symbols (crucifixes, hands, swords, flags) looks almost like a collection of still photographs, for the sepia tint is reminiscent of faded daguerreotypes. The only pronounced camera movement is a downward pan from the symbols of justice in the courtroom to the judge (a "falling" which will reappear throughout the movie as a complement to Michael's falls from imagined heights of success), but otherwise the sequence is virtually motionless, making no progress toward a resolution of the problems it sets forth and ending in a predictable tragedy.

The abrupt cut from the peasant's screaming face (as his hands are chopped off) to the title "Now," followed by Alan Price's hands on a piano, is an aesthetic leap of historical proportions. While the first sequence is limited to two colors and employs a narrative that follows an initial action to its complication and climax, this "modern" sequence, in full color, lacks any semblance of plot or story line; it is even termed "limbo" in the screenplay, and, as mentioned before, is more concerned with the *process* of filmmaking, the constantly changing perspectives here contrasting noticeably with the stable, staged, dramatic reality of the silent movie. Even Price represents an evolution of sorts from the peasant, since he makes a living with both his hands *and* his head.

For all of this relative freedom, however, we are nevertheless watching a controlled performance. There is no mistaking Anderson's authority here, as he keeps "on top of the action," holding scripts or music sheets and rising to confer with Price; he is, in effect, another overseer. This "modern" world is actually a rather enclosed realm of ideas, where Price puts forth ironic interpretations of Michael's adventures and where Anderson appropriately chooses to place the movie's credits. Alan is, obviously, more attuned to "reality" than Michael, who meets up with the band halfway through the movie and seems ignorant and "bumpkinish" in relation to their sophistication. But Alan's "knowledgableness," as Anderson terms it, is achieved by his rather extreme detachment throughout the film. True, he has an advantage from the start: "You feel perhaps that he has attained that attitude to life it takes the hero, Mick, the whole story to get to" (and Anderson adds that in this respect "the character of Alan is as near as the film gets to any kind of sentimentalism, because it's the nearest it gets to a straight portrayal of wisdom").[17] As the film cuts back and forth from Michael's tortuous struggles along the road to Alan's wise, relaxed renderings of songs about these struggles, it sets up an obvious contrast between the two characters: Michael keeps waiting for life to begin and for others to make sense of the world, while Alan knows that life is "Now" and eagerly takes responsibility for figuring things out for himself (and is, it should not be forgotten, *aware* that he is in a movie). Whatever attempts are made by the audience to identify with either character are probably exacerbated by this technique, for we are repeatedly jerked from Michael's story to Alan's reminders that Michael is, in essence, a clown who is going about things all wrong.

But how deeply can we identify with someone who only sits in "limbo" interpreting life, instead of living it? Who *is* Alan and how does he know so much? His detachment is, of course, highly Brechtian: that necessary distance which enables one to look coolly and objectively at what is going on. His music ("the nearest use in cinema to Brecht's use of music in *The Threepenny Opera*,"[18] claims Anderson), composed after the script was completed in accordance with Anderson's suggestions (which, for example, signified at certain

The presiding geniuses of O Lucky Man!: *(top) cinematographer Miroslav Ondricek (left) with Malcolm McDowell and Lindsay Anderson; (bottom) composer Alan Price.*

places that a "Song of . . ." was needed), accomplishes something unique in film. Although Alan plays the role of a musician, his music does not serve to develop his character or intensify emotion (the usual role of music). In purely Brechtian terms, his songs are indeed epic: they set forth the text, take up positions, and adopt attitudes. This is clear from the start of the film, as he sings the title song, whose lyrics suggest the course of Michael's tribulations:

> . . . If you've found the reason to live and not die—
> You are a lucky man!
> Preachers and poets and scholars don't know it,
> Temples and statues and steeples won't show it,
> . . . Takers and fakers and talkers won't tell you,
> Teachers and preachers will just buy and sell you,
> . . . You'll be better by far
> To be just what you are—
> You can be what you want
> If you are what you are—
> And that's a lucky man!

When the Rolling Stones kept recording "Sympathy For the Devil" in *One Plus One*, they were, as Godard well knew, creating consumer product. There was about as much artistic joy in their studio as in an IBM boardroom. But Alan's songs, and his energetic image, work toward—not against—a creative high. If "Sympathy For the Devil" ends up being some kind of radical dirge, "O Lucky Man!" is a victory cheer for the triumph of creativity over consumerism.

The Progress Through Illusion

After the limbo sequence, the camera tracks along a highway into the Imperial Coffee Company, coming to rest near a group of salesmen trainees, all dressed alike in white lab coats and hats, all perfect reflections of a mass-produced world. Is this the same company which tyrannized the workers of the first sequence? In fact, it hardly matters, for one colonial system pretty much mirrors another. Whether mercantile or scientific (or even religious), the imperialistic arrangements which pervade the film are, basically, means of separating management from labor, consumer from product, intellect from body. As a member of the trainee group, Michael functions well, for with his bourgeois desire to succeed in the corporate world, he sincerely believes in a hierarchy which rewards conformity. But as we see, the belligerent, crusaderlike rhetoric of his boss ("You will be our representatives in the front line. Each of you is going to have to prove himself on the battlefield of Sales") finds its apocalyptic end in the atomic explosion later in the movie, when nineteenth-century imperialism results in nuclear holocaust. No one seems to question the ends served by such attitudes; the trainees' lecture hall, in fact, is decorated with pictures of bullet-shaped objects and diagrams of ears, suggesting the only sense these trainees have use for, being taught to take in "the word" from their superiors.

The corporate disregard for individuality is illustrated by the decor of the chairman's office. Behind his desk hangs a painting of a dark-skinned woman holding a basket of coffee beans on her head. The painting is actually created from strips which revolve to reveal a map of England divided into sales regions; the message is clear: people, like land, are only "territory" to be won "on the battlefield of Sales." Accordingly, the chairman "gives" Michael a sales area along with directions and an "identity": "Now, here is your card: never travel without it. Your map, your compass, and your car keys. Now go out there and fight." The chairman's rhetoric reflects the problems of Michael's life, for whether it is sales, "the brotherhood of man," or even art, Michael can only view experience as something occurring "out there," in isolated spheres of regulated activity (Alan's next song, "Poor People," mocks this attitude in the line, "Just get out there and do it"). Believing himself to be on the road to success, he is actually trapped into repetition, having been chosen as a replacement for another salesman, just another face to fill "the great hole" in the Northeast.

Provided with a car, a map, and a compass, Michael now has a predetermined course to follow; his means of motion, direction of motion, and purpose for motion have all been decided by his superiors, as well as his new identity. The chairman hands Michael an apple, which, of course, presages a "fall," but not the traditional tumble from grace. Michael's greed is not really a problem compared with his chronic passivity and almost unconscious acceptance of slogans and directions from those "above" him. His "God" (the chairman, or, by extension, his belief in realms of controlled experience which have no connection with his immediate life) is his devil, since it dooms him to repetition. He has not developed any way of personally dealing with his environment, relying instead on an *a priori* system of responses, whether he is called upon to describe coffee, smile like a con man, or even have sexual relations.

As Michael drives to his new territory, he tunes his transistor radio to news broadcasts and public service lectures, always keeping the words of authority droning in his car. The radio, hanging from his rear view mirror, *is* his mirror of the world; he is more interested in changing stations than in looking around (showing just what a perfect product of the Imperial training sessions he really is). As a consequence, he rarely sees people approach him and does not (until the end of the movie) realize he is being observed; Monty, Mary Ball, security guards, and the vicar's wife all "ambush" him later on. As evidence that he is more attuned to sound than sight, Michael volunteers to be witness for a car crash he has not seen (because of a heavy fog, he has only heard the squealing tires and crashing metal). The police claim that they can see what has happened, although they come across the wreckage later than Michael. Each party wants to be a witness, but neither has seen the actual crash. As corrupt as they are, the police nevertheless correctly assess the situation when they threaten Michael: "Our word against yours." Michael's surprise shows his ignorance about his own attitude toward life, for he, like the police, has placed no value on direct experience so far.

Michael's immaturity is suggested by the cache of adolescent—even childish—paraphernalia he finds in his lodgings. Left behind by his predecessor at Imperial Coffee, the items include a teddy bear, a chest expander, a football jersey, and sex magazines. So preoccupied is Michael with his new toys that he does not see the mysterious lodger, Monty, enter his room, and looks up only when Monty says, "So you're the new rabbit. . . . You're the replacement are you?" This perceptive description of Michael as an experimental animal (and, ironically, an easily reproduced one) is lost on Michael, who pompously touts his virtues as a salesman.

Monty is something of a fairy-tale godfather, giving Michael a new set of clothes which he has apparently made himself. The gold suit fits its owner "perfectly": not surprising, for Michael is hardly differentiated enough to have an unusual body. In fact, he fits any set of clothes, for, like standardized parts for a standardized machine, the shirts and pants he finds in Patricia's closet later in the movie fit him "perfectly." The gold suit assumes magical implications by the strange arpeggio of music which accompanies our first vision of it, but its outrageous fashion would be appropriate only on a performer. It makes its final appearance on Michael at the cast dance, when, as a star's suit, it becomes a glittering symbol of Michael's awakening.

As Michael practices his sales pitch and winning smile before the mirror, Alan sings another song, the sequence cutting back and forth from the limbo of the band to Michael's room—the first time the two worlds have been "joined" on screen. During Alan's previous song, the opening maraca rattles were heard as part of Michael and Gloria's coffee-tasting ritual at company headquarters and the end of the song was heard as Michael drove across the moors. Gradually, it seems, the "timeless," "plotless" world of the musicians is being interwoven with Michael's systematized, highly rational world. While Michael thinks in terms of "ambition" and "technical knowhow" and delineates his universe by a company map of sales regions, the musicians appear unfettered by such concerns. The contrast is especially evident as we flash back and forth from Michael's desperate search for restaurant addresses and his anxious attempts to impress prospective buyers to the band's immersion in its music and casual acknowledgment of the camera. The futility of his career is mirrored in the deserted canteen at Amalgamated Steel, a bleak, Dickensian structure. Learning that five thousand men have been laid off for "redundancy," Michael makes no connections concerning his own job; he does not realize that hundreds of men could do his job with similar results. He even starts to identify himself corporately: "Travis, Imperial Coffee." Conformity is *not* rewarded in the long run, but Michael's company continues to employ men as interchangeable parts in its mechanical schemes to reap profits.

The next time the worlds of Michael and the band meet is in a visual collision, when the musicians' van nearly hits Michael as he escapes on a bicycle from the Millar Clinic, a collision which raises interesting questions about the movie's approach to the idea of "reality." While the band inhabits a relatively creative world, they may, nevertheless, seem more "real" to us by virtue of their first appearance as members of the filmmaking crew and familiarity with Anderson. Michael, on the other hand, inhabits a creative world by virtue of his status as lead character in the narrative, but his experiences may seem more "real" than the immobile music-making of the band. The visual unifying of the band with Michael, then, breaks down any categorization of the "worlds" of the movie; the ambiguity suggests that the movie is not simply a world of art set apart from experience—a world "out there"—but is, in essence, experience.

The Wakedale party Michael attends to "make contacts" is symptomatic of the highly regimented, unimaginative world he admires, for apparently the business and political leaders of the town gather every Tuesday night to watch stag movies and topless dancing. Art in this world is assigned the role of portraying predictable situations, for the movie shown at the party is just like thousands of others of its genre. The relegation of sexual excitement to a weekly backroom gathering reveals the sterility of a culture unable to merge its physical instincts and passions with everyday experience. The members of the audience are merely voyeurs, taking in vicarious sexuality, totally passive themselves (like Michael). As consumers of a type of "apathetic art" (or art Rollo May would term "schizoid"[19] in its avoidance of the anxiety involved in dealing with imagination and eroticism), the men have reduced vital activities to an unspontaneous formula. The stage performance entitled "Chocolate Sandwich" illustrates this beautifully, for the only active male in the place is the black "stud" on stage. The plantation workers have come in from the fields of the first sequence to satisfy the voyeuristic lust of the white men, only to be napalmed into submission by the end of the film. No series of images more concisely expresses the dualistic arrangements of Michael's world than that of the dissipated eyes of the town elders focused on the black man's sexual antics with the two white girls.

The emptiness of this life-style only appears glamorous to Michael. Despite all of the hints around him to *wake up* (his telephone number, for example, is *Wake*ly 4726, and he is living in *Wake*dale), he leaves town in the middle of the night, obeying garbled telephone orders from Imperial headquarters (orders which are cut off abruptly, leaving Michael connected to no one). Setting off for Scotland to "make contacts," he leaves his only physical contact, Mary Ball.

Appropriately, he arrives at a literal dead-end on the road. Throughout the trip, he only consults his maps and seems to have absolutely no instinct for direction or imagination about where he is going. He is even oblivious now to his radio, missing the discussion of Zen "illumination" which has particular relevance to Michael's situation. When it is obvious that his maps are of no use, he uses his binoculars, the first important use of his eyes since his midnight awakening at Mary Ball's house (which was the first in a series of awakenings). Although he looks beyond the fence which blocks his progress, he ignores the full panorama around him and therefore does not see the soldiers who come in jeeps and trucks. As usual, he hears the men before he sees them. Sound will continue to awaken him until he sees where he is, something he is completely baffled about now, for he cries out to the soldiers, "I'm only trying to find out where I am!" When the soldiers throw a black bag over Michael's head, they draw attention to the fact that he *is* in the dark, literally as well as figuratively.

When he is taken by the soldiers to the nuclear research lab, he leaves his confining room to explore the building. Instead of trying to find a way *out*, however, he climbs a stairway marked "Personnel Forbidden Beyond This Point," pushing farther *into* an already futile situation. While ignoring "orders" for the first time, he is nevertheless continuing to manifest a desire to "rise," to find an answer at the top of the stairs. As a cliché of the corporate world, "rising to the top" (recalling the coffee company's belief that for a good salesman "the sky's the limit") suggests one of the major problems raised in the film—disembodied knowledge, or, in political terms, the separation of management from labor. The debilitating effects of such a schismatic system are illustrated by the ironic skull-and-crossbones sign in the lab; it will reappear on the vats of "honey" shipped to Zingara and, as an X ray of a skull, on the walls of the Millar Clinic.

Blindfolded once again (for seeing part of a strange experiment in the lab), Michael is forced by his interrogators to confront his passivity, for while they seem determined to prove him a spy, he cries out, "I don't know anybody. . . . I don't know what I've done. I haven't done anything," statements applicable to not only his conduct throughout the movie but his ignorance that he has indeed been seeing "forbidden things." (He cannot even answer the question, "Do you realize where you are?") Refusing to sign a "confession," he is tortured by electric currents (in a pose reminiscent of the peasant in the first sequence, as his hands are strapped down), despite his protest that "I'm innocent. I haven't done anything." But his innocence is exactly what has landed him in this situation, for his childlike obedience has made him a perfect scapegoat; he can fill any role created by others, blending in all too well with his surroundings (his brown clothes match the walls and desks in the interrogation room, as they did the decor of the coffee company, Mary Ball's house, and the Wakedale Hotel; they even match the sepia tint of the first sequence, further linking Michael with the unlucky plantation worker). The pain inflicted on Michael by his inquisitors is, despite its sadistic nature, exactly what he needs: a literal shock to his system, a jolt of electricity to "spark" him out of his apathy.

"Falling" Toward Reality

The interrogators ask Michael a question which refers specifically to his "past:" "Was your Headmaster correct to expel you from school?" The question obviously pertains to McDowell's role in *If* . . . (but outrageously so—expulsion for *murder*?). Though he has the same appearance and name, the Michael of *O Lucky Man!* bears little psychological resemblance to the Michael (Mick) of *If. . . .* That the latter, an imaginative, aggressive boy who rebelled against authority and regimented behavior, would become a kowtowing, low-level salesman makes no sense psychologically. Anderson has, in effect, broken an assumed chain of causality by using the same character and actor while discarding psychological probability and narrative cause-and-effect. Perhaps this Michael is only a "replacement" for the previous Michael ("perhaps his cousin,"[20] Anderson offers), but the identity of Michael Travis remains uncertain. In a first step toward self-determination, however, Michael's identification with the Imperial Coffee Company is dropped after this episode. Defining himself in terms of a corporate world has gotten him nowhere, although he will continue to look for "success" until he finally exhausts his capacity for conformity.

Not only does Anderson destroy narrative causality in the interrogation scene, but he disrupts the linearity of progress essential to the bourgeois success story. The notion that success is an ascending spiral of events toward a mystical realm inhabited by those who have "made it" is undermined by the collapse of various power structures (here, the nuclear lab). The backfiring of atomic research, resulting in the explosions which destroy the lab, not only deflates the illusion of a controllable universe but closes the gap between intelligence and physicality. The holocaust intended for "enemies" explodes in the faces of its creators; those who build bombs finally confront the consequences of their activity. The uncontrollability of nature defeats its regulators and the illusion of power is just that: an illusion.

Michael's ultimate success as a camera subject depends on his movement away from these heights of illusory power toward concrete reality. Accordingly, after sliding down a steep hill to escape the atomic blasts and falling asleep on the ground, he will be awakened by church bells and beckoned toward another fall. The sunlit, idyllic valley Michael sees spread out below him seems untouched by the catastrophe he has just witnessed; in fact, his elevation above the valley suggests that the nuclear explosions have occurred in a "higher" realm, a stratum unrelated to that of the valley. Every time Michael descends from a pronounced elevation, he finds himself in a world out of touch with the one he has just left. Each descent takes him farther away from the airy heights of power and closer to the reality of physical existence. Only when he hits a literal rock bottom near the end of the movie is he freed from the habit of looking *upward* toward imagined centers of authority and forced to look *around* him. Until then, however, his blindness to his environment traps him a cycle of repetition, meeting the same faces over and over again. The reappearance of nearly every actor in the film as several different characters establishes human connections between the isolated worlds of his experiences, connections to which Michael, with his fragmented view of life, is oblivious.

Michael's semi-autism is revealed also by the blackouts, which appear repeatedly throughout the movie at the conclusions of episodes. By plunging us into utter darkness at the end of many scenes, Anderson stresses not only the dead-end nature of each system of thought represented in the adventure, but Michael's situation as well, as he gropes along, half-conscious and unaware of the discontinuity and unrelatedness of his world. (Several years after making *O Lucky Man!* Anderson said, "If I were free to, I would replace the black frames . . . with television commercials. It would be brilliant, helping to create that ironic juxtaposition between the idiocy of the real world and the film.")[21]

The valley community is just as isolated—psychically—as every other group of people we have seen so far in the film. The church Michael comes upon is so removed from atomic reality that the service becomes a monument to blindness. But as an old way of dealing with reality, the church operates under the same imperialistic regulations as the coffee company and the nuclear lab, subsuming the fruits of its labors under the auspices of a higher, abstract power. Although Michael is starving, the vicar's wife refuses to let him eat any of the sacrificial harvest ("That's *God's* food"), offering her breast instead. This scene was foreshadowed by the shot of Michael holding Becky the bar girl on his lap at the stag party in Wakedale, in which we saw only Becky's torso and Michael's enrapt, childlike face as he sucked on a bottle. While women constantly mother Michael, the men of the film are amazingly absent from any procreative activity. Their paternalism operates as imperialism, thus the separation of men into "head" figures and women into "body" figures deepens the divisiveness of the first part of the movie.

The idyllic peacefulness of the valley ends abruptly as Michael discovers the superhighway which runs by the rural fields. Such peacefulness, in view of its proximity to modern technology, seems artificial, dreamlike. Michael, in fact, has to run down a long slope to reach the highway—another descent from "ethereal" heights (reinforced by the downward pan of the camera as he walks through the woods). The romantic lifestyle of the valley, then, operates by excluding the rest of the world, by ignoring the realities of its environment, by behaving, in short, like Michael.

Michael is still willing to be manipulated—or at least guided—by others, though, for he follows the vicar's wife's directions to "go South," follows her children through the fields, and is given a ride not to the South but to the Millar Clinic, where he agrees to be a guinea pig for outrageous genetic experiments. A series of images in this sequence reflects not only Michael's situation in the movie but the nature of systems, such as Dr. Millar's, which are devoted to man's malleability in the name of an ever-efficient society. We first see Michael ordered into a wheelchair upon entering the clinic; although his superiors constantly press him into immobility, his movement here is completely dominated by the clinic staff, who wheel him about as if he were paralyzed. In a following scene, as Dr. Millar raves about the glory of the dinosaur, who "dominated this globe for one hundred forty million years," we see Michael sandwiched between stretchers, revolving anticlockwise around a steel arc. Unable to act or even react, he is molded into a repetitive mechanical action, turning *against* the movement of time. In the next scene, Dr. Millar expounds on the possible propagation of eight hundred million "manpower" in England if the seas were drained, for "no human being really needs more than seven and a half square feet to lead a really functional existence." The "mass production" of so many people, with no regard for their mobility, would result in a situation Michael ironically portrays as he rides a stationary bicycle, frantically exerting himself while going nowhere. In Dr. Millar's final appearance he talks of "falling in love, making love" as an "absurdly inefficient way of distributing random genes," while we see Michael in bed, wearing pajamas, being prepped for a computer-controlled genetic operation. The reproduction of Constable's *Cornfield* which hangs over his bed is a reminder, like the other landscapes which have appeared in the film (both painted and, like the rural valley, "real"), that the worlds Michael has encountered find no distinctive place for man in their schemes. The only paintings of humans we have seen so far have been generalized symbols of oppression and dominance (the brown plantation worker in the chairman's office and Queen Elizabeth in the nuclear lab). Accordingly, the highly perspectivized landscapes reflect the control of a rational, mathematical intelligence. When Michael makes his decision to break out of the Millar Clinic, the paintings around him will change from architectonic designs to im-

Some luckless moments: (top) Michael in the hands of the law; (bottom) Michael at the mercy of Dr. Millar.

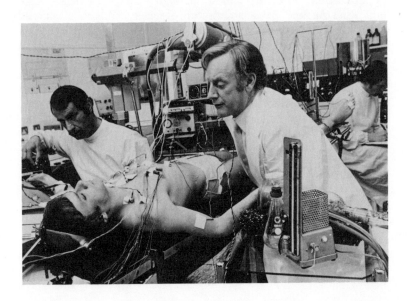

pressionistic compositions (namely, the Renoir paintings of individuals in Patricia's apartment and Sir James's house).

When physical self-preservation finally saves Michael (jerking him
awake during Dr. Millar's instructions to sterilize him), he stops only
once to see for himself the consequences of the doctor's world view: a
convulsing creature with the head of a boy and the body of a pig, the
issue of the "new genetics." The desire to control life has ended in the
destruction of human life, the reduction of man to simply a head with
no capacity for procreation or movement, catalyst enough for
Michael to dive out a window, his third fall from the heady heights of
intellectual control.

The Frame-Up

Appropriately, his most positive act yet—literally breaking out of a
corrupt, dehumanizing institution—results in his collision with the
band. By rejecting Dr. Millar's system, he has made his first really
independent decision and for the first time seems truly unusual to
people, an absurd "Golden Wonder" (as the band calls him), rather
than a reflection of his superiors' desires or a carbon copy of others.
Michael's seduction by Patricia in the van marks his entrance into the
upper-class world of Sir James and high finance (Patricia's name
indicating the new "patrician" stratum of society). When Patricia and
Michael breakfast on the roof of her London flat (an appropriate place
to renew his fascination with heights), neither she nor her objects can
hold his attention when he sees Sir James's skyscraper, the tallest
building on the horizon. While Patricia has the capacity to grow
beyond her social limitations, calling Michael "old-fashioned" and
"hopelessly conventional" for his declaration of bourgeois ambition
to get "right to the top," she is hardly more revolutionary or nonconformist than her father, Sir James. She practices her own form of
imperialistic acquisition by stealing art objects from him and by
collecting boyfriends ("She's making a study of us," Alan tells
Michael). She mingles with the lower-class band members as a
"kick," for she goes home "when I get bored," and seems inextricably
woven into the fabric of upper-class life (as borne out by her later
appearance in evening regalia in her father's study).

Patricia and her father, however, represent more than aristocratic
ruthlessness; they personify the divisions created by imperialistic
lifestyles. Parent and progeny never appear on the screen together
(recalling the vicar's visual dissociation from his children in the valley

church episode); indeed, they manifest no affection for each other at any point. Sir James is all intellect and manipulation, with no connection to the physical world. He collects art as a symbol of his wealth, not from any innate response to the works; his home is somewhat like the museums John Dewey called "memorials of the rise of nationalism and imperialism"[22] in its accumulation of aesthetic booty. The only connective tissue in this world is purely abstract and mercantile; the flesh and bone have been discarded years ago.

Left alone in the flat by Patricia and the band, Michael does not explore his new environment or go sightseeing in London, but heads instead straight "for the top," to the most detached place in town: Sir James's penthouse office (reminiscent of the elevated office of Imperial Coffee's chairman). The office is a black and white study in abstraction; the only color in the room is found in the large, gold, tooth-shaped sculpture, a droll symbol of acquisition (like its ancestor in Erich von Stroheim's *Greed*). Reflected here is a world of precision and absolute control. Appropriately, Sir James's desk faces a blown-up black and white aerial photograph of London; as he sits at his desk he can peer down at the world from a position of domination and isolation.

Just as he drives peasants off their land in South America, so does he drive Professor Stewart to his death, for the distraught scientist has been cast aside by his employer. The only words we hear Sir James speak to the professor while Michael waits in the reception room are "No!" and "Impossible." The professor, whose "revolutionary concept" has just been rejected by Sir James, drags Michael out of his chair in a plea for help and then leaps to his death from the window, carrying the office assistant with him—an obvious parallel of Michael's previous plunge from the Millar Clinic window. Ironically, the professor "is" Dr. Millar (one of the recurring faces in the movie); his singular interest of no value to his superior, the obsessed scientist has become unhinged in his final incarnation, his mania for manipulation having driven him insane.

Although Sir James gives the professor a perfunctory memorial service, no mention is made of the dead assistant. Apparently, replacements are easy to find for such a position, for Michael "lucks into" another role as lackey. Sir James simply hands Michael his briefcase and Michael, still willing to follow, marches out the door behind his new boss, ignoring all visible signs of doom.

The meeting at Dr. Munda's house, which Michael and Sir James attend, is similar to the Wakedale party, for here we find a collection

of superficially respectable political and business leaders brought
together for an evening's worth of dubious entertainment. As conspirators in exploitation, the guests have a mutual interest in repres-
sing the people of Zingara, of whom Dr. Munda is the president, and
creating a totally functional, servile poulation (and the fact that the
mayor of Wakedale "is" now Dr. Munda is a hilarious linkage of the
two characters, as well as a reminder that Dr. Munda is not really
black—a "white Negro," in essence). The travelogue-type movies
shown by the Zingaran contingent are, like the stag film in Wakedale,
manipulated images, pictures predicated on a generalized view of
reality and portraying the submission of one entity to another. The
first film, narrated by Michael's predecessor at Imperial Coffee,
Oswald (who has been reduced to a disembodied voice in the dark),
perfectly reflects the imperialistic mentality which pervades Sir
James's world. We first see Zingaran natives performing their "age-
old rituals"; this scene cuts to "the patrons of our holiday lodges,"
who sit in bourgeois splendor atop their penthouse terraces enjoying
the "picturesque entertainment." The two worlds of native and
patron are finally brought together in a vision of "the future": a gaudy
painting of smiling Caucasians being catered to by equally happy
natives.

Mrs. Naidu's film and attendant commentary attempt to extol the
virtues of the Zingaran labor situation, but her very appearance
undercuts the efficacy of her message, for she is not an African or
Third World native of indistinct nationality (as the others are), but an
Indian, dressed in sari and sandals, an ironic reminder of the failure
of British imperialism. As her film shows, by segregating its sexes
into distant work camps, the Zingaran government offers a sterile,
thoroughly oppressed haven for "the foreign investor" (who is shown
lounging beside a luxurious swimming pool). The rape of Zingara
appears complete, for the natives are portrayed as simply a black
mass, undifferentiated, unindividuated, and unnamed—nearly inhuman. But for those who dare rebel and threaten the stability of
foreign investment, Colonel Steiger, the compleat Fascist, offers
visual proof of their fate: total physical mutilation and destruction. A
series of still photographs provides evidence that the colonel can
effectively destroy any life in his path.

This meeting, then, is the culmination of the concerns of the
business and technological worlds we saw in the first part of the
movie. All of the rhetoric and research has been integrated to form an
overpowering destructive force bent on the domination and, if neces-

sary, elimination of human beings in the name of a higher power (money or country). If, as Member of Parliament Basil Keyes says at the end of the scene, "Power creates the man," Michael and those around him are visual contradictions of the statement, more robotlike than vital, either all intellect (like Basil and Sir James), all body (like the courtesan and, at this point, Michael), or nearly inhuman (like Oswald). Power, as the colonel's slides illustrate, destroys rather than creates.

Since Michael is still imitating others at this point, he, of course, is doomed to failure. The perfect "fall guy" for the plottings of others, he is the replaceable element in the cabal. Oblivious to the implications of his job (sending napalm—or "honey"—to Zingara), he is as usual blind to most of what is going on around him (like, for example, the stares of Sir James's chauffeur through the rear view mirror). Yet he finds that he does not exist in the vacuum of nonidentity any longer. Sergeant Beevers studies Michael's face at the airport and can later point to him and say, "That's the man." Michael signs a form for Beevers and this time (as compared with his previous signings of forms) connections are made between his signature and his face. Just as Basil warns him, "Don't leave any fingerprints," Michael is no longer a ghostlike figure and must face the consequences of his apathy and passivity.

Michael's frame-up consists of his agreeing to be a "witness" at the signing of illegal documents. (The term "frame-up," like "fall guy," suggests an important element in Michael's story, for he is indeed "framed" by his inability to break out of the movie's intended restrictiveness at this point. Interestingly, Patricia is often involved in cutting out expensive paintings from their frames, an activity which parallels Michael's eventual breakout from authority.) Just as in the car crash episode, he claims to be a witness for something he has not seen, and is now promptly arrested by the Fraud Squad (a most fitting reminder of Michael's fraud as a witness all through the movie). His arresting officers (the same ones who appeared at the car crash) not only beat him, but throw a black coat over his head, casting Michael once again into the dark.

The miscarriage of justice at his trial is flagrant, but ironically so. The judge, dressed in a Santa Claus–type robe, is a rather salacious soul (as was the Santa of the stag film in Wakedale), more interested in satisfying his own appetite than in serving others. Michael, of course, believes in Santa Claus, or at least in a world which drops wealth and success in the laps of those who simply "believe." However, in his chosen world of acquisition and plunder, Santa is just as selfish and egotistical as the rest of the characters, moving from a figure of lust to one of age and hostility. His rhetorical question, "Was this the action of an innocent?" raises a crucial issue, however. Michael is indeed guilty of an almost inhuman passivity, certainly a crime in the world of film, which finds its material in motion, activity, tension, and rebellion—all components of a creative process. He is, by extension then, a threat to the cinematic imagination, for he has repeatedly ended up in repetitive situations, trapped in a cycle of stimulation-and-response, never initiating activity or exploring his environment (his two black eyes in this scene are a testament to his blindness). The titles "Guilty!" "Unlucky!" and "Justice," interspersed with shots of Michael's face, parallel those of the peasant's sequence, and function as ironic indictments of Michael as a camera subject. He is, in essence, guilty of doing nothing (and here is where the critical comparisons to Watergate figures becomes most relevant). The movie, however, does not end with Michael's punishment, as the melodrama of the first sequence does, but eventually resolves Michael's problem in a manner impossible in the social realism of the peasant's story.

The Final Illusion

The use of titles as a transition device to Michael's prison life not only introduces us to his new world of books and words (and distances us further from his "psyche"), but foreshadows the problem Michael will have in relating his social rhetoric to reality (the righteous descriptions of jail sentences are interset with miserable images of the jails themselves). He tells the prison governor, "I've been thinking . . . I've read books, and I see things differently now," but this is only partly true, for he has indeed been thinking and reading, but does not see much differently than before. He is, in fact, so caught up in books that he does not notice the warder watching him through a peephole, the eye looking strangely like an eye focusing through a camera lens (another reminder that Michael is being observed without realizing it).

As his new reading matter indicates (Gorky, Bertrand Russell, Lenin), Michael's interests now center on an idealism about humanity he will find hard to maintain, for he has become as enamored of his new theories as he was of the imperialistic attitudes in his "coffee days." He is still looking outside himself—to higher authorities—for his "answers," but ideas developed in such isolation do not have a chance in the hopeless world he will encounter in the East End. Although Michael now has a mind, he still has no internal motivation for living, no self-discovered insights; in short, he has not yet opened his eyes to the world around him, preferring instead to adopt the views of "great thinkers." The governor's comment, "You have eyes like Steve McQueen, did anyone ever tell you that?" while foreshadowing Michael's realization of his own stardom, is the last of a series of compliments concerning his eyes; he will soon live up to these remarks, especially Dr. Millar's description of Michael's eyes as "interesting," when he auditions for Anderson. For the time being, though, he still sees life as a realm "out there," for as he tells the governor, "I just want to get out there and learn to be a proper human being." Rather than setting out anew from jail, however, he leaves with an address from the warder, once more accepting directions from a superior.

When we first see Michael in the East End, he is framed by a wall bearing the graffiti, "Revolution is the Opium of the Intellectuals." This reworking of the Marxist slogan is a fitting comment on Michael's new mentality, for if religion sedates the masses, revolution—or rather, the theorizing about revolution which elevates it to an abstract sacrament—pacifies intellectuals, for those who propound ideals rarely bear the physical consequences of their theories. Michael, with his talk of "we're all there is, only man exists . . . it's the only truth," reflects an intellectualism which generalizes human beings into collective masses. While certainly an advance over his former apathy toward life (and at least he recognizes Patricia—he can make *some* connections now), this new idealism imbues experience with preconceptions about how people should behave, and clouds Michael's *per*ceptions with spurious *con*ceptions. Trying to participate in helpful activity, he volunteers as a social worker, yet he begs for directions ("What shall I say? What shall I do?"). He does not follow the advice of the salvationist to "just be yourself," for having consistently mistaken adopted and directed behavior for his own personality, Michael has no "self" on which to rely.

The characters in the derelict area are more than "fallen men"; they are inhabitors of a bombsite, the detritus of imperialism. Michael's lecture to them on "man! . . . What a marvellous word!" receives taunts to "go back to school . . . back to Nanny . . . join the army." The derelicts finally push him off a ledge, their response to someone whose head is lost in space. Michael has hit the nadir of his experiences, the literal rock bottom; his fall is complete.

Rebirth and Illumination

Surprisingly, he lives (or is reborn), for we next see him hobbling through a dark alley, a black shadow against the street lights. Although dark, the street is alive with more activity and color than we have ever seen in the movie. Now stripped of all his preconceptions about life, Michael wanders alone, without a projected goal, without illusions, resembling, in fact, the quintessential existential man. He, of all people, is approached by the "pig boy" (now fully human) to "try your luck" and "be a star." Showing up at Anderson's audition, he notices familiar faces in the audience. He stares at Patricia and several young men who have appeared in other scenes; he even "senses" their presence, turning around in his chair to meet their stares. No longer do people spot him first; he makes connections himself. When Michael is called forth to pose for pictures, Anderson leaves his schoolmaster's podium and walks down to him (a descent as important for Anderson as Michael's were for him). The clapper board reading "O LUCKY MAN!, Scene 755" which snaps in front of Michael is the ultimate dissolution of vicarious experiences, for the movie he auditions for is not a hypothetical enterprise to occur at some point in the future ("out there"), but the ongoing process of his life.

Michael is told to hold books and a machine gun, both props from his previous role (or "life") in *If . . .* ; he obeys Anderson's orders, yet, when commanded to look "more aggressive" he aims the gun at Anderson. When told to smile, Michael, for the first time ever, rejects a direct order. His smile has been his knee-jerk tool for winning acceptance; he has practiced it to impress coffee buyers and "contacts," wearing it finally as an idiotic symbol of his empty-headedness when, after being framed, he flashes a trusting grin at Sir James. He is now incapable of smiling "without a reason." His question to Anderson, "What's there to smile about?" reflects not only his miserable experiences, but his new awareness of others' misery (made clear in his scrutiny of the tragic news headlines on the street). He sees the failure of all of his systems of belief as the end of his world, and indeed it is, but Michael's newly discovered logic leads him to conclude that without a system, a world "out there" to conquer, he is nothing. Smiling from impulse rather than calculation is beyond him at this point. His rejection of the director is, therefore, both positive and negative, for it establishes him as an "actor" rather than a passive tool of others and as a person who has developed both a mind and a body. But Michael has yet to develop his imagination or sense of humor, to explore new possibilities of existence around him. By whacking him on the head (with the script!), Anderson has chosen an appropriate response, for it is Michael's head which has proved an obstacle to his growth. He literally has some "sense" knocked into him, a phenomenon recalling both the Gestalt dictum "Lose your mind and come to your senses" and the Zen "illumination" which was discussed on the radio as Michael drove through Northumberland (even Anderson has dubbed himself a possible "Zen master"[23] here). As Michael stands dazed, his senses seem to awaken, for as he stares right at the camera, a half-smile appears on his face. While this smile may be seen as obedience to Anderson or as a relapse into his old mechanical response to commands, in light of the movie's absorption in the process of moviemaking, it is the culmination of self-consciousness: an awareness (even if partial) both of himself as the camera's subject and, as Anderson has said, "of the correct way of relating to his experience, to everything that has happened to him."[24]

Michael's realization of the camera proves his awakening and is an act of self-awareness which does more than reinforce the cliché that "it's all just a movie." His discovery, in fact, disintegrates whatever notions about the separation of art from life we may bring to movies. The actors may all be conspirators in their menacing reappearance in Michael's life, but they only repeat unfortunate adventures as long as he is blind to what is going on. Once he realizes he is in a movie, his cycle of repetition is broken and the audition hall is magically transformed into a massive celebration dance. Unlike Sir James, who commands an aerial view of London from his penthouse, Michael will never attain a stable perspective (or one which implies that the perceiver is "on top of the action"). Either falling from strata to strata, emerging from the darkness of blackouts, or, finally, dancing around a room, Michael progresses simultaneously toward extinction as a personality (with its implication of psychological history) and birth as an image. As the audition scene makes clear, his identity *is* his image: the struggle to attain anything else negates the movie itself. This, of course, constitutes the "self-reflexivity" of the film, for by finally being aware that he sees and *is* seen, Michael acknowledges the futility of ever achieving a superior, authoritative view of anything.

The scrawled message Michael stands in front of at the beginning of the dance sequence could serve as a coda for the film: "It's all true."

The cast dance is a celebration in which all of the divisions and classes of the previous scenes are broken down by the appearance of an assortment of costumes from every caste and the "uncharacteristic" behavior of each actor. Even Alan Price no longer proffers wry comments on Michael's life, but performs music to accompany, not define, others' motion. Anderson, too, breaks out of his role as a director by embracing Michael and disappearing into the crowd, an acknowledgment that his creation is now self-propelled, moving forward without his guidance, and, in effect, has been born. Anderson's action signifies film (and, by extension, life itself) as the one activity explored in the movie which is not dependent upon imperialistic divisiveness and intellectual control for its success.

Even the camera seems freer here, panning in circles, taking in the full panorama instead of "falling." This circular motion, of course, reflects the concept of cycles—or unity—as opposed to linearity (which is undermined all through the film). As Alan sings here:

And it's around and round and round and round and round we go,
And it's around the world in circles turning,
Earning what we can. . . .

But one of the most interesting facts about the ending is that the camera itself is in the center of the action, revolving on its own axis instead of tracking *around* a subject (as in the ending of Herzog's *Aguirre, Wrath of God*, for instance). It is the camera—not Michael, not Anderson—which becomes the obvious medium of perception, the center of the film. We have, in essence, witnessed a "revolutionary" transformation of the concept of movies, then, from finished product ("Once Upon a Time") to self-conscious production (limbo) to liberated perception itself. The "Now" of the second sequence becomes the "Now" of Michael's life and the "Now" of the entire film.

The concept of luck, so pervasive as a theme throughout the movie, comes to suggest, in the context of Michael's experiences, the random luck of birth itself. Michael has been chosen by the camera as its subject by chance and, like Anderson, who claims that he became a film director "by luck,"[25] Michael has the good fortune to realize his possibilities in life, to be, in Anderson's words, "plunged once again into the flux of creation,"[26] to be, in short, "born." As the camera lens irises-in on Michael's dancing body, it once again selects him as its subject, catching him in a final image before he dances out of the frame for good. In contrast to the stooped, servile peasant of the first sequence, Michael has evolved into a standing, individuated person, physically reaching out to world of color, complexity, and motion.

7

Afterword:
British Possibilities,
The Descending Spiral?

IN THE SPRING of 1980 I visited Lindsay Anderson in London, where he was in the midst of directing another David Storey play, *Early Days*, at the National Theatre. While he has not directed a film since the American Film Theater's *In Celebration* in 1975, he was tentatively planning to film Alan Bennett's *The Old Crowd*. His production of the play for London Weekend Television (which I was able to see) is in some ways a video extension of *O Lucky Man!*, with television itself coming under as much metaphoric scrutiny as film does in the earlier work (the television sets and studio cameras appear as unexpectedly as the audition scene in *O Lucky Man!*). Anderson calls the taped play "rather Buñuelesque," but its style, tone, and (for the lack of a more succinct term) reflexivity mark it as distinctly "Andersonian." I regret only having seen it once, and it is our loss that plans to sell the work to American cable companies have not crystallized (at the time of writing the British unions had not accepted an agreement for remuneration). A study of Anderson's work is not complete without some kind of analysis of a production like this, especially since, as Anderson notes, "Television has provided an opportunity for work and a certain amount of experimentation which the British Cinema has always been too conventional to permit," not suffering from "the commercial straitjacketing of television in the U.S." (As an interesting sidelight, however, Anderson also claims that "commercialism apart, television by its very nature [or its social nature] is vowed to conformism, and so I don't see any really mature or considerable tradition of filmmaking emerging from TV.")[1]

Anderson's other plans included the publication of his John Ford book, the possible direction of a film for Orion Pictures (*Empire*, from a script prepared with Ted Tally, about the 1857 Indian Mutiny), a collaboration with David Sherwin on a film project entitled *Brittania Hospital*, and the possible direction of *Dress Gray* (from a script by

Gore Vidal). The problems of funding are more oppressive than ever; as he points out, nearly everything he directed after *This Sporting Life* was backed by American money, 'and now Americans are not interested in financing British production in the way they were ready to do in the sixties and early seventies."[2]

Although Anderson claims he probably does not have "the immense energy"[3] to undertake another massive film project, one cannot help but be struck by his unusual intensity and enthusiasm, and feel that if the economic and cultural situation were different, he would be bounding about on a set at this minute, creating another masterpiece (something, he has hinted, of "greater satirical or innovative charge" than what is currently offered most directors). He did formulate a project about a British hospital "which could have been developed into a pretty fierce, comprehensive and outrageous kind of satire, but the response of the British to ideas of this kind is to label them 'parochial,' and therefore not financable."[4]

It seems ironic that a study which begins with the "descending spiral"[5] of British films should come full circle. So many factors account for this dismal situation: the failure of the Free Cinema directors to gain a permanent foothold in the industry, the failure of the British to invest in their most successful productions—in short, to recall Anderson's words, "the failure of national self-belief." If Anderson is correct that the British "have no real interest or conviction in native subjects,"[6] we are left with a little over a decade's worth of sparkling cultural originality—and very little hope for the future. Anderson's films remain the brightest examples of the potential of British cinema. They deal honestly and intimately with their social environment, yet transcend it to capture, in E. M. Forster's words, "that peculiar pushful quality" of universal works of art: "The excitement that attended their creation hangs about them, and makes minor artists out of those who have felt their power." [7]

Notes and References

Chapter One

1. All quotations are from "Get Out and Push," in *Declaration*, ed. Tom Maschler (Port Washington, N.Y., 1957), pp. 141, 146, 142.
2. Ibid., p. 145.
3. Letter to the author, 29 August 1979.
4. Ibid.
5. Paul Gray, "Class Theatre, Class Film: An Interview with Lindsay Anderson," *Tulane Drama Review* 11 (Fall 1966): 124.
6. Letter to the author, 29 August 1979.
7. Letter to the author, 20 July 1979.
8. Letter to the author, 29 August 1979.
9. "Sport, Life and Art," *Films and Filming* 9, no. 9 (1963): 18.
10. Letter to the author, 29 July 1979.
11. Alexander Walker, *Hollywood UK: The British Film Industry in the Sixties* (New York, 1974), p. 23.
12. Anderson, *Sight and Sound* 24, no. 2 (1954): 108.
13. G. Roy Levin, "Lindsay Anderson," in *Documentary Explorations: 15 Interviews with Film-makers* (Garden City, N.Y., 1971), p. 71.
14. Letter to the author, 29 July 1979.
15. Gavin Lambert, Introduction to Anderson's John Ford monograph, *Cinema* 6, no. 3 (1971): 22.
16. Anderson, "Stand Up! Stand Up!" *Sight and Sound* 26 (Autumn 1956): 64.
17. Levin, p. 68.
18. Anderson, "Get Out and Push," p. 144.
19. Anderson, "John Ford: A Monograph," *Cinema* 6, no. 3 (1971): 136.
20. Anderson, "Get Out and Push," p. 144.
21. Maurice Merleau-Ponty, "The Film and the New Psychology," in *Sense and Non-Sense*, Tr. H. L. Dreyfus and P. L. Dreyfus (Evanston: Northwestern University Press, 1964), p. 58.
22. Letter to the author, 20 July 1979.

23. Alan Lovell and Jim Hillier, *Studies in Documentary* (New York, 1972), p. 145.

24. Walker, p. 27.

25. Ibid., p. 26.

26. Gavin Lambert, "Free Cinema," *Sight and Sound* 25, no. 4 (1956): 174.

27. Letter to the author, 29 July 1979.

28. Peter Cowie, "An Interview with Lindsay Anderson," *Film Quarterly* 17, no. 4 (1964): 12.

29. Letter to the author, 20 July 1979.

30. Elizabeth Sussex, *Lindsay Anderson* (New York, 1969), pp. 31–32.

31. "Angles of Approach," *Sequence*, no. 2 (Winter 1947), pp. 5–6.

32. Quoted in Anderson, "Stand up! Stand Up!" p. 64, and "French Critical Writing," *Sight and Sound* 24, no. 2 (1954): 105.

33. Philip T. Hartung, "Foreign Climes, Foreign Crimes," *Commonweal* 78 (19 August 1963): 480.

34. "Sport, Life and Art," p. 18.

35. Walker, *Hollywood UK*, p. 28.

36. "Sport, Life and Art," p. 18.

37. "French Critical Writing," p. 105.

38. Ibid.

39. Guy Flatley, " 'We Have to Make Our Own Acts of Courage,' " *New York Times*, 1 July 1973, sec. 2, p. 9.

40. Lambert, Introduction to Ford Monograph, p. 22.

41. "Angles of Approach," p. 7.

42. "Get Out and Push," pp. 139–40.

43. "Stand Up! Stand Up!" p. 67.

44. "The Last Sequence of *On The Waterfront*," *Sight and Sound* 24 (January–March 1955): 129.

45. Review of *Birth of a Nation*, *Sight and Sound* 22, no. 3 (1953): 130.

46. "Perspectives at Cannes," *Sight and Sound* 24, no. 1 (1954): 6.

47. "Cannes 1953," *Sight and Sound* 23, no. 1 (1953): 20.

48. "Notes From Sherwood," *Sight and Sound* 26, no. 3 (1956–1957): 159–60.

49. Laurence Kitchin, *Mid-Century Drama* (London: Faber and Faber, 1960), p. 193.

50. "Get Out and Push," p. 144.

51. Letter to the author, 20 July 1979.

52. Levin, p. 69.

53. Letter to the author, 20 July 1979.

54. Lovell and Hillier, p. 156.

55. "Get Out and Push," pp. 145–46.

56. Levin, p. 68.

57. Sussex, p. 44.

58. Levin, p. 69.

59. Joseph Gelmis, *The Film Director as Superstar* (Garden City, N.Y.: Doubleday, 1970), p. 106.

60. Ibid., p. 104.

61. Ibid., p. 105.

62. Letter to the author, 20 July 1979.

63. Bertolt Brecht, "The Epic Theatre and its Difficulties," in *Brecht on Theatre: The Development of an Aesthetic*, ed. and trans. John Willett (New York: Hill and Wang, 1964), p. 23.

64. Letter to the author, 20 July 1979.

65. Kenneth Tynan, "Bertolt Brecht," in *Essays in the Modern Drama*, ed. Morris Freedman (Boston: D. C. Heath, 1964), p. 143.

66. "Sport, Life and Art," p. 16.

67. Robert Bolt, *A Man For All Seasons* (London: Heinemann, 1960), act 1, p. 39.

68. "Angles of Approach," p. 6.

69. Merleau-Ponty, *Sense and Non-sense* p. 58.

70. "The Current Cinema—*The Quiet Man*," *Sight and Sound* 22, no. 2 (1952): 25.

71. Review of *The Last Hurrah*, *Sight and Sound* 28, no. 2 (1959): 93.

Chapter Two

1. Gelmis, p. 97.

2. "Only Connect: Some Aspects of the Work of Humphrey Jennings," *Sight and Sound* 23, no. 4 (1955): 181.

3. Levin, p. 67.

4. Ibid, p. 66.

5. Ibid., pp. 70, 63.

6. Ibid., p. 67.

7. Lovell and Hillier, p. 18.

8. Anderson, "Only Connect," p. 186.

9. Sussex, p. 40.

10. Sussex claims this in her book, p. 17.

11. "Only Connect," p. 182.

12. "John Ford: A Monograph", p. 135.

13. Ibid.

14. "Panorama at Cannes," *Sight and Sound* 26, no. 1 (1956): 18.

15. Gelmis, p. 97.

16. "A Possible Solution," *Sequence*, no. 3 (Spring 1948), p. 9.

17. Sussex, p. 39.

18. Gelmis, p. 97.

19. Sussex, p. 40.

20. Rudolf Arnheim, "Lindsay Anderson: Free Cinema II," *Film Culture*, 4, no. 2 (1958): 11.

21. Review of *Wagonmaster*, *Sight and Sound* 19 (December 1950): 333.

Chapter Three

1. Walker, p. 174.
2. "Sport, Life and Art," *Films and Filming* 9, no. 9 (February 1963): 15.
3. Walker, p. 129.
4. Robert Vas, "Arrival and Departure," *Sight and Sound* 32, no. 2 (1963): 57.
5. "Sport, Life and Art," p. 17.
6. Letter to the author, 29 August 1979.
7. Letter to the author, 20 July 1979.
8. "Sport, Life and Art," p. 16.
9. David Storey, *This Sporting Life* (New York: Avon, 1960), p. 67.
10. Ibid., p. 163.
11. John Russell Taylor, *David Storey* (Harlow, Essex: Longman Group, 1974), p. 6.
12. Martha Duffy, "An Ethic of Work and Play," *Sports Illustrated* 38, no. 66 (1973): 66.
13. "The Last Sequence of *On the Waterfront*," *Sight and Sound* 24 (January-March 1955): 128.
14. David Storey, p. 139.
15. Ibid., p. 163.
16. Gelmis, p. 109.
17. C. G. Jung, "Marriage as a Psychological Relationship," in *The Collected Works of C. G. Jung*, trans. R. F. C. Hull, ed. Herbert Read, Michael Fordham, Gerhard Adler, William McGuine, Bollingen Series 20, vol. 17 (Princeton: Princeton University Press, 1954), p. 197.
18. David Storey, p. 254.

Chapter Five

1. Guy Flatley, " 'We Have to Make Our Own Acts of Courage,' " *New York Times*, 1 July 1973, sec. 2, p. 17.
2. Evelyn Waugh, *Decline and Fall* (New York: Dell, 1934), p. 245.
3. Elizabeth Sussex, "Lindsay Anderson's New Film," *Times* (London), 29 November 1968, p. 14.
4. Letter to the author, 29 August 1979.
5. Walker, p. 404.
6. David Robinson, "Anderson Shooting *If . . .*," *Sight and Sound* 37 (Summer 1968): 131.
7. Letter to the author, 29 August 1979.
8. "Get Out and Push," p. 149.
9. Sussex, p. 14.
10. Kitchin, p. 195.
11. "Get Out and Push," p. 137.
12. "They Call it Cricket," *Declaration*, p. 151.

13. "Alfred Hitchcock," *Focus on Hitchcock*, ed. Albert J. LaValley (Englewood Cliffs, N.J.: Prentice-Hall, 1972), p. 49; originally published in *Sequence* 9 (Autumn 1949).

14. Letter to the author, 29 August 1979.

15. Flatley, p. 9.

16. Gelmis, p. 108.

17. "Notes For a Preface," *"If . . .": A Film By Lindsay Anderson and David Sherwin* (New York: Simon and Schuster, 1968), p. 10.

18. Letter to the author, 29 August 1979.

19. "Perspectives at Cannes," *Sight and Sound* 24 (July–September 1954): 6.

20. Ivan Butler, *The Making of Feature Films: A Guide* (Harmondsworth: Penguin, 1971), p. 65.

21. Letter to the author, 29 August 1979.

22. Waugh, p. 392.

23. Anderson and Sherwin, *"If . . . ,"* p. 57.

24. Sussex, p. 14.

25. Taylor, p. 92.

26. Gelmis, p. 106.

27. David Robinson, "Stripping the Veils Away, *Times* (London), 21 April 1973, p. 7.

28. Sussex, p. 84.

29. Gelmis, p. 107.

30. Ibid., p. 108.

31. Anderson and Sherwin, p. 167.

32. Robinson, "Stripping the Veils Away," p. 7.

33. "Notes For a Preface," p. 13.

34. Sussex, "Lindsay Anderson's New Film," p. 14.

35. Robinson, "Anderson Shooting *If . . . ,*" p. 131.

36. Osborne, p. 58.

37. "Notes For a Preface," p. 12.

Chapter Six

1. Letter to the author, 19 September 1979.

2. Letter to the author, 20 July 1979.

3. Martin Esslin, *Brecht: A Choice of Evils* (London: Eyre and Spottiswoode, 1959), p. 111.

4. Robinson, p. 7.

5. Although this is my interpretation of the shot, the screenplay offers the following support: "Mick, dazed, lifts his head. His eyes find the camera" (David Sherwin, *"O Lucky Man!"* [London: Plexus, 1973], p. 188).

6. Anderson has described *O Lucky Man!* as a "fairy tale" or "magic story" (from a lecture given by Anderson at the University of Florida, April 1975; on videotape at the University of Florida Library).

7. Robinson, p. 7.

8. Ibid.

9. Ibid.

10. Anderson to the author, April 1980.

11. Sherwin, "Diary of a Script," in *"O Lucky Man!"*, , p. 21.

12. Ibid.

13. Robinson, p. 7.

14. James Delson, *"O Lucky Man!" Take One* 3 (May–June 1972): 30.

15. Robinson, p. 7.

16. Delson, p. 30.

17. Robinson, p. 7.

18. Mark Carducci, "From Theater to Film . . . Lindsay Anderson," *Millimeter* 3, no. 1 (1975): 24.

19. Rollo May, *Love and Will* (New York: Dell, 1964), p. 95.

20. Robinson, p. 7.

21. Carducci, p. 24.

22. John Dewey, *Art and Experience* (New York: Capricorn, 1934), p. 8.

23. Robinson, p. 7.

24. Ibid.

25. From the aforementioned University of Florida lecture.

26. Letter to the author, 19 September 1979.

Chapter Seven

1. Letter to the author, 29 August 1979.

2. Ibid.

3. Anderson to the author, April 1980.

4. Letter to the author, 29 August 1979.

5. Phrase first used by Anderson in "British Cinema: The Descending Spiral," *Sequence*, no. 7 (Spring 1949), pp. 6–11.

6. Letter to the author, 29 August 1979.

7. E. M. Forster, "Does Culture Matter?" in *Two Cheers for Democracy* (London: Edward Arnold, 1951), p. 116.

Selected Bibliography

Primary Sources

1. Interviews (arranged chronologically)

COWIE, PETER. "An Interview With Lindsay Anderson." *Film Quarterly* 17, no. 4 (1964): 12–14. Conducted just after the release of *This Sporting Life*, the interview provides excellent, though brief, background information on Anderson's views of the theater and film scene in England in the late 1950s and early 1960s.

GRAY, PAUL. "Class Theatre, Class Film: An Interview With Lindsay Anderson." *Tulane Drama Review* 11 (Fall 1966): 122–29. This interview gives an interesting view of Anderson in the mid-1960s: angry, unconventional, and highly critical of so-called "liberal" British films of the era.

SUSSEX, ELIZABETH. "Lindsay Anderson's New Film." *Times* (London), 29 November 1968, p. 14. An excellent interview at the time of *If . . .*'s release. Anderson discusses the film's "relevance" to current politics and his view of anarchy.

GELMIS, JOSEPH. "Lindsay Anderson." In *The Film Director as Superstar*. Garden City, N.Y.: Doubleday, 1970. Pp. 93–110. Probably the best general interview with Anderson. Gelmis's intelligent questions prompt highly informative and fascinating responses from Anderson concerning politics; the making of movies; and specific aspects of his documentaries, *This Sporting Life*, and *If . . . .*

FLATLEY, GUY. " 'Home': The Playwright: 'I Never Saw a Pinter Play.' " *New York Times*, 29 November 1970, sec. 2, pp. 1, 5. A superficial, but humorous, interview with Anderson and David Storey during the run of *Home* in New York. The interview reveals a good deal of the interaction between the director and playwright and, despite their facetiousness, we get an interesting view of their attitudes toward drama (and interviewers).

LEVIN, G. ROY. "Lindsay Anderson." In *Documentary Explorations: 15 Interviews with Film-makers*. Garden City, N.Y.: Doubleday, 1971. Pp. 62–71. Along with Gelmis, Levin asks the most intelligent questions of all the interviewers on record. A highly useful discussion of Anderson's attitudes toward politics and film, politics and the artist, and documentary film in general.

ROBINSON, DAVID. "Stripping the Veils Away." *Times* (London), 21 April 1973, p. 7. An excellent interview concerning all aspects of *O Lucky Man!* and some aspects of Anderson's aspirations as a director.

FLATLEY, GUY. " 'We Have to Make Our Own Acts of Courage." *New York Times*, 1 July 1973, sec. 2, pp. 9, 17. Rather interesting, if superficial, interview concerning *O Lucky Man!* American politics, and general attitudes toward movies.

2. Essays on Cinema (arranged chronologically)

"Angles of Approach." *Sequence*, no. 2 (Winter 1947), pp. 5–8. One of Anderson's first essays, it contains a description of why he dislikes "middlebrows," "artistic patriotism," and utilitarianism, as well as his definition of the duty of the artist.

"A Possible Solution." *Sequence*, no. 3 (Spring 1948), pp. 7–10. An interesting attack on the British film industry and the Grierson school of documentary-making.

"British Cinema: The Descending Spiral." *Sequence*, no. 7 (Spring 1949), pp. 6–11. Anderson criticizes the British films of the year for their pomposity, dullness, and cliché-ridden scripts and bemoans the fact that "somehow the exciting, stimulating films fail to materialise."

"Only Connect: Some Aspects of the Work of Humphrey Jennings." *Sight and Sound* 22, no. 4 (1955): 181–86. An excellent summation of Anderson's approach to documentary-making, including an implicit attack on the Grierson school.

"The Last Sequence of *On The Waterfront*." *Sight and Sound* 24 (January–March 1955): 127–30. Anderson criticizes Kazan's film for a variety of highly interesting reasons and, in the process, reveals his own view of responsible, imaginative film direction.

"John Ford: A Monograph." *Cinema* 6, no. 3 (1971): 23–36. Originally written in 1955. Anderson's long, highly detailed essay describes his reasons for admiring Ford and his reactions to specific movies.

"Stand Up! Stand Up!" *Sight and Sound* 26 (Autumn 1956): 63–69. One of Anderson's most famous essays, it provides the best view of his critical reasoning turned loose on dull-witted and misinformed film critics.

"Get Out and Push." In *Declaration*. Edited by Tom Maschler. Port Washington, N.Y.: Kennikat Press, 1957. Pp. 137–60. Anderson's contribution to this late 1950s collection of reflections on British art and culture by major critics of the time is one of his best. A funny, fascinating, severe attack on British complacence and a plea for his culture to tackle the realities of the mid-twentieth century.

"Sport, Life and Art." *Films and Filming* 9, no. 9 (1963): 15–18. Anderson's last major essay, it contains information on the making of *This Sporting Life*, his approach to the novel, and his views of film art in general (including his famous point that the artist's "duty is to be a monster").

3. Books

About John Ford. . . . London: Plexus, 1981. Book not available for review at time of publication.

Making a Film: The Story of "Secret People." 1952. Reprint. New York: Garland, 1977. The book is Anderson's detailed, day-to-day account of the making of the 1951 film. Treating all aspects of production, it is most interesting from the point of view that Anderson himself was learning a great deal, for his films are certainly more accomplished than this one.

Secondary Sources

1. Bibliographies

SILET, CHARLES P. *Lindsay Anderson: A Guide to References and Resources.* Boston: G. K. Hall, 1979. The only complete and detailed bibliographic guide to works about and by Anderson. The book is an invaluable research aid and is extensively researched.

2. Books

LOVELL, ALAN, and HILLIER, JIM. *Studies in Documentary.* New York: Viking, 1972. One of the best books on British documentary work, it contains a great deal of historical information on Free Cinema and Anderson's role in the British cinema.

SUSSEX, ELIZABETH. *Lindsay Anderson.* New York: Praeger, 1969. A comprehensive look at Anderson's films up to *O Lucky Man!,* his career, and his writings. All relevant biographical data is contained in this book as well as the most detailed examination of his Free Cinema work.

WALKER, ALEXANDER. *Hollywood UK: The British Film Industry in the Sixties.* New York: Stein and Day, 1974. Walker's book provides one of the most comprehensive examinations of the films of the era and places Anderson's career in the context of the social and cultural trends of the time. A good deal of the book is devoted to Anderson's influence and films, and as such is a valuable research aid for anyone interested in either Anderson or the sixties in Britain.

3. Essays

CUNNINGHAM, FRANK R. "Lindsay Anderson's *O Lucky Man!* and the Romantic Tradition." *Literature/Film Quarterly* 2, no. 3 (1974): 256–61.

The essay is one of the few truly interesting attempts to work with the film's complexities. The emphasis on romanticism is not labored and what emerges is a refreshing look at Travis's progress through illusion.

DURGNAT, RAYMOND. "*O Lucky Man!* Or: The Adventures of a Clockwork Cheese." *Film Comment* 10 (1974): 38–40. The "essay" is really a humorous pastiche of all kinds of cultural, film history, and social references which have some relation to *O Lucky Man!* Despite the superficiality, the piece does mention some interesting connections worth researching.

FARBER, STEPHEN. "Before the Revolution." *Hudson Review* 22, no. 3 (1969): 469–73. Perhaps the most thoughtful essay on *If . . .* (at least for its time), which avoids the clichés and looks at the film from the perspective that it "dares to mock *both* antagonists in the battle at Generation Gap."

LAVERY, DAVID. "*O Lucky Man!* and the Movie as Koan." *Literature/Film Quarterly* 3, no. 1 (1980): 35–40. An interesting discussion of the "cinematic labyrinth" of the film and its Zen aspects.

LOVELL, ALAN. "Brecht in Britain–Lindsay Anderson [on *If . . .* and *O Lucky Man!*]." *Screen* 16, no. 4 (1975–1976): 62–86. A transcription of a symposium on Brechtian techniques and leftist politics as they relate to Anderson's work. While the participants' political biases work against their arriving at truly original insights, the piece is nevertheless interesting for its particular perspective.

ROBINSON, DAVID. "Anderson Shooting *If . . . .*" *Sight and Sound* 37, no. 3 (1968): 130–31. An interesting look at the problems of shooting the film; some fascinating comments by both Anderson and David Sherwin are contained in the essay.

VAS, ROBERT. "Arrival and Departure." *Sight and Sound* 32, no. 2 (1963): 56–59. Reprinted in *Renaissance of the Film*, ed. Julius Bellone (London: Collier-Macmillan, 1970), pp. 277–88. One of the best essays on *This Sporting Life*, it attempts to deal with the uniqueness of the film (or its non-"angry" characteristics). A highly perceptive piece, especially considering its time of publication, when so many critics were obsessed with generalizing about "working class films."

Filmography

MEET THE PIONEERS (Richard Sutcliffe Ltd., 1948)
Producers: Desmond and Lois Sutcliffe
Cinematographer: John Jones and Edward Brendon
Editors: Lindsay Anderson and Edward Brendon
Art Adviser: Eric Westbrook
Music: Arranged by Len Scott
Commentary: Spoken by Lindsay Anderson
Running time: 33 minutes
No U.S. distribution or rental

IDLERS THAT WORK (Richard Sutcliffe Ltd., 1949)
Producer: Richard O'Brien
Cinematographer: George Levy
Music: Ralph Vaughan Williams and Aaron Copland
Continuity: Lois Sutcliffe
Unit Assistants: Bill Longley, Geoff Oakes, Ernest Slinger, and George
    Wilby
Commentary: Spoken by Lindsay Anderson
Running time: 17 minutes
No U.S. distribution or rental

THREE INSTALLATIONS (Richard Sutcliffe Ltd., 1952)
Producer: Desmond Sutcliffe
Cinematographer: Walter Lassally
Additional cinematography: John Jones
Assistant cameraman: Desmond Davis
Editor: Derek York
Music: Aaron Copland, Gillis, and Khatchaturian; Conveyor Boogie by Alan
    Clare (piano) and Johnny Flanagan (drums)
Sound recording: Charles Green
Production manager: John Exley
Unit assistant: Vincent Young
Commentary: Spoken by Lindsay Anderson

Running time: 28 minutes
No U.S. distribution or rental

WAKEFIELD EXPRESS (The Wakefield Express Series Ltd., 1952)
Producer: Michael Robinson
Cinematographer: Walter Lassally
Music: Performed by Snapethrope and Horbury Secondary Modern School;
    band music by Horbury Victoria Prize Band
Production assistant: John Fletcher
Commentary: Spoken by George Potts
Running time: 33 minutes
No U.S. distribution or rental

THURSDAY'S CHILDREN (World Wide Pictures, A Morse Productions,
    1953)
Co-director: Guy Brenton
Coauthor: Guy Brenton
Cinematographer: Walter Lassally
Music: Geoffrey Wright
Commentator: Richard Burton
Cast: Children from the Royal School for the Deaf, Margate
Running time: 20 minutes
U.S. Availability: Museum of Modern Art, New York

O DREAMLAND (A Sequence Film, 1953)
Cinematographer: John Fletcher
Assistance: John Fletcher
Music: Frankie Laine's "I Believe;" "Two Glasses and Hot Toddies" and
    Muriel Smith's "Kiss Me, Thrill Me"
Running time: 12 minutes
U.S. Rental: Grove Films, New York

TRUNK CONVEYOR (Richard Sutcliffe Ltd., National Coal Board, 1954)
Producer: Desmond Sutcliffe
Cinematographer: John Reid
Assistant Cameraman: Gerry Godfrey
Editor: Bill Megarry
Assistant editor: James Vans Collina
Music: Songs by Bert Lloyd; concertina, Alf Edwards; Guitar, Fitzroy
    Coleman
Production manager: Peter Woodward
Commentator: Lindsay Anderson
Running time: 38 minutes
No U.S. distribution or rental

GREEN AND PLEASANT LAND, HENRY, THE CHILDREN UP-STAIRS, A HUNDRED THOUSAND CHILDREN (National Society for the Prevention of Cruelty to Children, Basic Film Productions, 1955) ④
Producer: Leon Clore
Scripts: Lindsay Anderson
Cinematographer: Walter Lassally
Running times: *Henry*, 5½ minutes; the others, 4 minutes each.
No U.S. distribution or rental

£20 A TON, ENERGY FIRST (National Industrial Fuel Efficiency Service, Basic Film Productions, 1955)
Producer: Leon Clore
Cinematographer: Larry Pizer
Production manager: John Fletcher
Running times: Each about 5 minutes
No U.S. distribution or rental

FOOT AND MOUTH (Central Office of Information for the Ministry of Agriculture, Fisheries and Food, A Basic Film Production, 1955)
Producer: Leon Clore
Script: Lindsay Anderson
Cinematographer: Walter Lassally
Editor: Bill Megarry
Technical adviser: J. C. Davidson
M.R.C.V.S. Production manager: Philip Aizlewood
Commentator: Lindsay Anderson
Running time: 20 minutes
No U.S. distribution or rental

EVERY DAY EXCEPT CHRISTMAS (Ford of Britain, A Graphic Production, 1957)
Producers: Leon Clore and Karel Reisz
Cinematographer: Walter Lassally
Music: Daniel Paris
Recording and Sound Editor: John Fletcher
Assistants: Alex Jacobs, Brian Probyn, and Maurice Ammar
Commentator: Alun Owen
Running time: 40 minutes
U.S. Availability: Museum of Modern Art, New York

THIS SPORTING LIFE (Independent Artists, A Julian Wintle/Leslie Parkyn Production, 1963)
Producer: Karel Reisz
Screenplay: David Storey, based on his novel of the same name

Cinematographer: Denys Coop
Camera operator: John Harris
Editor: Peter Taylor
Assistant editor: Tom Priestley
Art director: Alan Withy
Set dresser: Peter Lamont
Dress designer: Sophie Devine
Music: Composed by Roberto Gerhard, conducted by Jacques-Louis Monod
Sound editor: Chris Greenham
Sound recording: John W. Mitchell and Gordon K. McCallum
Casting: Miriam Brickman
Production manager: Geoffrey Haine
Assistant director: Ted Sturgis
In charge of production: Albert Fennell
Cast: Richard Harris (Frank Machin), Rachel Roberts (Mrs. Hammond),
    Alan Badel (Weaver), William Hartnell (Johnson), Colin Blakely
    (Maurice Braithewaite), Vanda Godsell (Mrs. Weaver), Arthur Lowe
    (Slomer)
Running time: 134 minutes
U.S. Rental: Continental Films, Elk Grove Village, Ill.; available also at the
    Library of Congress

THE WHITE BUS (United Artists, A Woodfall Film Presentation, 1966)
    (originally part of the trilogy *Red, White and Zero*)
Executive producer: Oscar Lewenstein
Associate producer: Michael Deeley
Screenplay: Shelagh Delaney, based on her short story of the same name
Cinematographer: Miroslav Ondricek
Editor: Kevin Brownlow
Art director: David Marshall
Music: Misha Donat
Sound editor: John Fletcher
Sound recording: Peter Handford
Casting director: Miriam Brickman
Assistant director: Kip Gowans
Production manager: Jake Wright
Cast: Patricia Healey (Girl), Arthur Lowe (Mayor), John Sharp (Macebearer),
    Julie Perry (Conductress)
Running time: 46 minutes
U.S. Rental: United Artists, New York

THE SINGING LESSON (RAZ DWA TRZY) (Contemporary Films,
    Warsaw Documentary Studios, 1967)
Chief of production: Miroslaw Podolski
Cinematographer: Zygmunt Samosiuk

Editor: Barbara Kosidowska
Song arranger: Ludwik Sempolinski
Piano accompaniment: Irena Klukowna
Sound editor: Henryk Kuzniak
Sound recording: Malgorzata Jaworska
Assistant director: Joanna Nawrocka
Cast: Piotr Fronczewski (singing "The Coat"), Anita Przysiecka and Marian
   Glinka (singing "Big Beat"), Aniceta Raczek (singing "A Lullaby—For
   Those Who Wait"), Waldemar Walistak (singing "Sunshine Street"),
   Andrzej Nardelli (singing "Sweet Peas"), Joanna Sobieska and Andrzej
   Seweryn (singing "Oh, Miss Sabina!")
Running time: 20 minutes
No U.S. distribution or rental

IF . . . (Paramount, A Memorial Enterprises Film, 1968)
Producers: Michael Medwin and Lindsay Anderson
Screenplay: David Sherwin, from the original script "Crusaders" by Sherwin
   and John Howlett
Cinematographer: Miroslav Ondricek
Cameraman: Chris Menges
Editor: David Gladwell
Assistant editors: Ian Rakoff and Michael Ellis
Production designer: Jocelyn Herbert
Music: Composed and conducted by Marc Wilkenson; "Sanctus" from the
   "Missa Luba" (Philips recording)
Sound recordist: Christian Wangler
Casting director: Miriam Brickman
Assistant director: John Stoneman
Cast: Malcolm McDowell (Mick Travis), David Wood (Johnny), Richard
   Warwick (Wallace), Christine Noonan (The Cafe Girl), Rupert Webster
   (Bobby Philips), Robert Swan (Rowntree), Hugh Thomas (Denson),
   Peter Jeffrey (Headmaster), Arthur Lowe (Mr. Kemp), Graham Crow-
   den (History Master).
Running time: 112 minutes
U.S. Rental: Paramount; available also at the Library of Congress

O LUCKY MAN! (Warner Brothers, A Memorial Enterprises Film, A SAM
   Production, 1973)
Producers: Michael Medwin and Lindsay Anderson
Screenplay: David Sherwin, from an original concept by Malcolm McDowell
Cinematographer: Miroslav Ondricek
Music: Composed and performed by Alan Price, with Colin Green (guitar),
   Dave Markee (bass guitar), Clive Thacker (drums)
Editors: Tom Priestley and David Gladwell
Associate Producer: Basil Keys

Production designer: Jocelyn Herbert
Art director: Alan Withy
Sound editor: Alan Bell
Casting: Miriam Brickman
Cast: Malcolm McDowell (Michael Travis), Ralph Richardson (Monty, Sir
    James), Rachel Roberts (Gloria Rowe, Madame Paillard), Arthur Lowe
    (Mr. Duff, Charlie Johnson, Dr. Munda), Helen Mirren (Patricia),
    Graham Crowden (Professor Millar, Professor Stewart, Meths Drink-
    er), Alan Price (Alan), Peter Jeffrey (Factory Chairman, Prison Gov-
    ernor), Mary Macleod (Mary Ball, Vicar's Wife)
Running time: 166 minutes (from an original 186 minutes)
U.S. Rental: Warner Brothers; available also at the Library of Congress

IN CELEBRATION (Ely Landau Organization, Inc. and Cinevision Ltee.,
    an rbc films presentation, in association with the American Film Thea-
    ter, 1975)
Executive Producer: Otto Plaschkes
Producer: Ely Landau
Cinematographer: Dick Bush
Editor: Russell Lloyd
Screenplay: David Storey, based on his play of the same name
Cast: Alan Bates (Andrew), James Bolam (Colin), Brian Cox (Steven), Bill
    Owen (Mr. Shaw), Constance Chapman (Mrs. Shaw)
Running time: 131 minutes
U.S. Rental: Paramount; available also at the Library of Congress.

Index

Aguirre, Wrath of God (Herzog), 148
Amarcord (Fellini), 103
American Film Theater, 26, 60, 151
Anarchism, 33, 36, 37; (in *If . . .*) 95, 118–20
Angry Silence, The (Green), 58
"Angry" movement, 21, 23, 29
Arnheim, Rudolph, 53
Arnold, Matthew, 29

Bates, Alan, 58
Beatles, The, 85
Bennett, Alan, 38, 151
Berliner Ensemble, 29, 38
Billy Liar (Schlesinger), 58
Bolt, Robert, 39
Brando, Marlon, 31, 58
Brecht, Bertolt, 29, 37, 123, 128
Brechtian techniques (in Anderson's films), 38, 39, 54, 89, 103, 105, 123, 124, 125, 130
Bringing Up Baby (Hawks), 104
Brittania Hospital, 151
Burton, Richard, 47

Cahiers du Cinema, 30
Cannes Film Festival, 32, 95
Chabrol, Claude, 27
Constable, John, 138
Cooke, Alan, 27
Crusaders, 94
Cubism (in *Every Day Except Christmas*), 53

De Sica, Vittorio, 32
Declaration, 32

Decline and Fall (Waugh), 93, 108
Delaney, Shelagh, 84, 87
Dewey, John, 141
Drabble, Margaret, 84
Dress Gray, 151

Early Days, 151
Easy Rider (Hopper), 93
Empire, 151
Epic theatre, 38, 54, 105
Every Day Except Christmas, 28, 35, 36, 44, 48, 52–54, 88, 90

Fellini, Federico, 49, 79, 103
Finney, Albert, 58, 94
Ford, John, 23, 24, 32, 40, 48, 49, 54, 151
Forster, E. M., 24, 152
Four Hundred Blows, The (Truffaut), 96
Fragonard, Jean-Honore, 88

Godard, Jean-Luc, 130
Goretta, Claude, 27
Greed (von Stroheim), 141
Grierson, John, 22, 45, 46
Griffith, D. W., 31

Harris, Richard, 58, 67
Herzog, Werner, 148
Hitchcock, Alfred, 101
Howlett, John, 93

If . . ., 22, 24, 27, 36, 37, 48, 50, 61, 78, 80, 83, 85, 87, 88, 93–121, 124, 135, 136, 146
"If" (poem), 120
In Celebration, 26, 34, 35, 60, 84, 151

169

Jennings, Humphrey, 46, 47
Jung, C. G., 79

Kazan, Elia, 31
Kind of Loving, A (Schlesinger), 58
Kipling, Rudyard, 120

La Strada (Fellini), 79
Laine, Frankie, 48, 51
Lambert, Gavin, 23, 24, 28, 30
Langer, Suzanne, 99
Lassally, Walter, 48
Lodger, The (Hitchcock), 101
London Weekend Television, 151
Look Back in Anger (Richardson), 29, 38, 57
Lowe, Arthur, 85

McDowell, Malcolm, 39, 124, 125, 135
Man For All Seasons, A, 39
Manet, Edouard, 88
March to Aldermaston, 34, 44, 46, 51
Marxism: Anderson's relationship with, 33, 38, 46; in *If . . .* , 95; in *O Lucky Man!*, 123, 145
May, Rollo, 134
Mazzetti, Lorenza, 28
Memorial Enterprises, 94
Merleau-Ponty, Maurice, 27, 39
Momma Don't Allow (Richardson and Reisz), 28
Morgan: A Suitable Case for Treatment (Reisz), 21

National Film Theatre (London), 21, 28
National Theatre (London), 151
Neorealism, 27, 28, 49
New Left, 33
New Wave, 19, 20, 27, 57, 58, 59
Novello, Ivor, 101

O Dreamland, 28, 35, 44, 46, 48, 49–52, 53, 54, 83
O Lucky Man!, 21, 24, 27, 35, 36, 38, 39, 44, 54, 61, 78, 80, 84, 85, 89, 90, 103, 107, 116, 117, 118, 120, 121, 123–49, 151
Old Crowd, The, 38, 151
On the Waterfront (Kazan), 31
One Plus One (Godard), 130
Osborne, John, 20, 32, 59, 99, 118, 120

Oxford University, 22
Oxford University Film Society, 22

Paramount Pictures, 94
Picaresque (in *O Lucky Man!*), 125–26
Playtime (Tati), 84
Polanski, Roman, 27
Pollock, Jackson, 53
Price, Alan, 89, 126, 127, 130, 133, 140, 148

Ray, Nicholas, 94
Reisz, Karel, 27, 28
Renoir, Auguste, 140
Renoir, Jean, 40
Richardson, Tony, 27, 28, 29
Roberts, Rachel, 61
Robin Hood (television series), 32
Rodin, Auguste, 102
Rolling Stones, The, 130
Room at the Top (Clayton), 58

Saturday Night and Sunday Morning (Reisz), 21, 58, 59
Sequence, 22, 23, 27, 30, 31
Sherwin, David, 93, 94, 120, 124, 151
Sight and Sound, 22, 28, 32
Singing Lesson, The (*Raz Dwa Trzy*), 24, 36, 44, 83, 85, 89–91
Storey, David, 26, 34, 59, 60, 84, 151
Strawberry Statement, The, 93
Sutcliffe, Desmond, 22
Sutcliffe, Richard, Ltd., 22

Tally, Ted, 151
Tanner, Alain, 27
Taste of Honey, A (Richardson), 58
Tati, Jacques, 84
This Sporting Life (film), 21, 24, 26, 28, 30, 31, 34, 35, 36, 37, 38, 39, 55, 57–80, 83, 84, 87, 95, 97, 106, 107, 152
This Sporting Life (novel), 34, 59, 63, 75
Threepenny Opera (Brecht), 128
Thursday's Children, 35, 36, 43, 44, 47, 48, 49, 51, 90
Together (Mazzetti), 28
Truffaut, Francois, 27

Venice Film Festival, 52

Vidal, Gore, 152
Vigo, Jean, 103, 104
Von Stroheim, Erich, 141

Wagonmaster (Ford), 54
Wakefield Express, 22, 28, 35, 43, 46–49, 60, 84, 88
Walker, Alexander, 30, 58
Waugh, Evelyn, 93

We Are the Lambeth Boys (Reisz), 28
White Bus, The, 24, 35, 36, 37, 48, 50, 83–89, 95, 103
"White Bus, The" (story), 84, 87

Zavattini, Cesare, 32
Zen (elements in Anderson's films), 21, 39, 126, 134, 147